Big Easy
Cocktails

Big Easy
Cocktails

Jazzy Drinks and Savory Bites from New Orleans

Jimmy Bannos and John DeMers

TEN SPEED PRESS
Berkeley | Toronto

Acknowledgments: I want to thank Annamarie, my wife, my rock, and Jimmy and Anjelica, the fourth generation going into this business. Thanks as well to my business partners: George, Patty, Bob, and Karen; my restaurant managers Steve, Ed, Ruben, and Whitney, along with my bartenders Mike, Erin, Lyle, Bones, and Harold. At Ten Speed Press, my gratitude goes out to Phil Wood, Dennis Hayes, and Meghan Keeffe. A big thanks to my coauthor John, the best anybody could ever have. Finally, I need to thank my past and present staff for making my dream of Heaven on Seven a reality, our customers for validating our faith every single day, and the incredible city of New Orleans for inspiring me twenty years ago. —Jimmy Bannos

Ten Speed Press
Box 7123
Berkeley, California 94707
www.tenspeed.com

Distributed in Australia by Simon and Schuster Australia, in Canada by Ten Speed Press Canada, in New Zealand by Southern Publishers Group, in South Africa by Real Books, and in the United Kingdom and Europe by Airlift Book Company.

Cover and text design by Catherine Jacobes
Food and drink styling by Dan Becker
Prop styling by Catherine Jacobes and Annabelle Breakey

Library of Congress Cataloging-in-Publication Data
Bannos, Jimmy.
Big easy cocktails : jazzy drinks and savory bites from new orleans /
Jimmy Bannos and John DeMers.
p. cm.
Includes index.
ISBN-13: 978-1-58008-719-3 (pbk.)
ISBN-10: 1-58008-719-1 (pbk.)
1. Cocktails. 2. New Orleans—Social life and customs. I. DeMers, John, 1952–II. Title.
TX951.B23 2006
641.8'740976335—dc22   2005027967

Printed in China
First printing, 2006
1 2 3 4 5 6 7 8 9 10 — 10 09 08 07 06

PREFACE

It is the most important truth of this book on the cocktail culture of New Orleans that the city's genius for celebration grows not from any illusion that life is easy but from the fact that life is hard. Not just hard, mind you—the way life anywhere might be hard, might require us to work and sacrifice for our jobs, our homes, and our families. No, life in New Orleans has been built for 300 years on the remarkable ease with which life can take away *everything* it gives, can sweep away dreams and fond illusions, can steal the legacies of not only individuals but also generations. For all those around the world who recently watched our beloved Big Easy struggle through times that weren't easy at all, this greatest truth of New Orleans existence is as plain it is ever has been. As plain as it ever *can* be.

We believe that the genius for celebration found uniquely in New Orleans is not merely the party atmosphere, not simply the Mardi Gras mentality that attracts millions of visitors every year. We believe it's a way of looking at life, at fate and at fortune, that draws profoundly on the losses of three centuries. After all, the French Quarter was destroyed by fire twice in its early years, to be reborn during the reign of Spain and end up looking less like Paris and more like Old San Juan. In recent years, New Orleanians have seen fires devastate two of our most historic structures, the Cabildo on Jackson Square where the Louisiana Purchase was signed, dragging the licentious territory kicking and screaming into the prudish United States; and the Fair Grounds, site of the annual New Orleans Jazz and Heritage Festival and America's oldest racecourse. Inherent in these highly public losses was a reflection of highly private ones—betrayals, reversals of fortune, sickness, and death. If you find these truths debilitating, if they drive you to your bed in sadness and fear, then you are not anybody's idea of a New Orleanian. Keep our city as your destination for brain-dead spring break and think about it—think about *us*—no longer.

A true New Orleanian knows only too well that there is plenty to mourn and more than a little to fear. All of our best celebrations balance darkness and light, sorrow and joy, sin and redemption—this is a much too Catholic town not to. If you don't understand that, you understand nothing. A true New Orleanian—fueled, consoled, strengthened, and inspired by the sacrifices of the city's past—lives suspended between the deep resignation that there's nothing we can do and the deep conviction that there's so much we must do. This is the hopelessly tangled enigma that is New Orleans, as the city knows more fully now than at any time in its collective memory. As you'll see in all the pages that follow, this is how we really drink. This is how we really live. This is who we really are.

contents

❝ In this sign thou shalt conquer. I promise to abstain from all intoxicating drinks except used medicinally and by order of a medical man; and to discountenance the cause and practice of intemperance. ❞

—THE VERY REV. THEOBALD MATHEW
(1790–1856)

INTRODUCTION

With all due respect to his holiness—or at least his soberness—Reverend Mathew, we say, "Welcome to the only city we know with an entire tour devoted to 'the cause and practice of intemperance.'" While it might strike some as long overdue (and others as utterly redundant), the pleasure-loving city known as the Big Easy is now offering a tour dedicated to walking, stalking, stumbling, or crawling through the French Quarter in search of strong drink. If, in the course of taking this tour, reading this book, or sampling these spirited recipes, you feel the sudden need for the right reverend's "order of a medical man," we suggest you bring your own M.D. along for the ride.

Let us take care of some business right off the bat. While we certainly don't countenance temperance as a movement, and we agree with most that Prohibition was an inept and destructive way to address a "social ill," we actually *do* both preach and practice moderation. New Orleanians strive for moderation far more than the typical tourist or conventioneer—you know who you are, staggering beneath the wrought iron and bougainvillea, your neck bent beneath the weight of Mardi Gras beads when the actual date is as far from the next Mardi Gras as it is from the last. Unlike you, we live here and actually have to get up and go to work in the morning—a lot earlier than you'll probably start searching for your first steaming mug of café au lait.

Now, a few words about Heaven on Seven, the restaurants that give life to all these wonderful cocktails and snacks daily. Created wholecloth by Chef Jimmy Bannos after his passionate encounter with the people, culture, and cuisine of New Orleans, the four locations of Heaven on Seven embody everything the Crescent City believes about eating and drinking. They simply embody it in and around the equally great dining city of Chicago. As a third-generation restaurateur, Jimmy knew the real thing when he tasted Creole and Cajun food in New Orleans in the 1980s, taking home the lessons he learned from legends like Paul Prudhomme. These lessons apparently worked in Jimmy's case, since his restaurants are beloved as places where "it's Mardi Gras every day" and where just about every meal kicks off with a dark and steaming bowl of gumbo. In Chicago, as in New Orleans, the current renaissance of the great American cocktail has opened many doors to creativity, with the results not only what you taste at Heaven on Seven but now can prepare at home.

In this book, we'll do several things at once. First, we'll share with you the unique history over the course of more than 300 years that made New Orleans the city it is today. Remember that what you may see as license we understand as tolerance, a trait honed to perfection in this melting-pot port where anybody and everybody who arrived here from Europe or the Caribbean or washed on down the muddy Mississippi was forced to form an alliance. We'll also share with you our love of the cocktail itself, a many-splendored creation believed to have been born here (none of the theories about the possible role of some hotel bar in New York makes a lick of sense to us, and they are therefore not entertained here) and understood by all to have been elevated here from mere libation to lifestyle. And finally, we'll share with you our love of terrific cooking, here expressed in a host of recipes for snacks and appetizers that capture the authentic flavors of New Orleans.

Most of all, we'll share with you an attitude and a worldview that the French phrase *joie de vivre* can only hint at. After all, the New Orleanian approach to alcohol, food, music, dancing, and just about everything this side of professional golf is based not on tireless joy, but rather on the

awareness of inevitable sorrow. It's true. Over three centuries, New Orleanians have seen almost everything they treasure (from their French Quarter to their cathedral to their beloved Fair Grounds racetrack) burn right to the ground. Once you've spent more than a long lost weekend in New Orleans, it's impossible to forget that time passes quickly. Milestones pass, from birth to marriage to procreation to death, reminding us always that love is, at the same moment, both eternal and anything but.

Real life doesn't just drive us to drink here in New Orleans. It's also what keeps us sober, enjoying and embracing the moment, those small

flowerings of joy in all their forms. We understand too well that neither they nor we will be here forever.

A Jigger of Early Times

People, places, and things are woven together like a tapestry in the story of how New Orleans became the birthplace of the cocktail. People, as usual, are the catalysts, the movers and, when it comes to famous cocktails, the shakers as well. Indeed, the invention of the cocktail required two elements uniquely possessed by New Orleans: the traditional use of the French language and its repeated mangling by those rubes often dismissed here as *les Américains*. The story begins with a man named Antoine Peychaud, who escaped the violent slave rebellions on the Caribbean island of Santo Domingo in the late eighteenth century—the upheaval that doubled this city's population with newcomers that all spoke French and were raised on the island's African rhythms and religious tradition we know as "voodoo." Described alternately as a druggist, a pharmacist, and, most romantically, an apothecary, Peychaud was clearly a fellow who'd be at home with a chemistry set.

Peychaud operated a now-legendary pharmacy on Royal Street in the French Quarter in the 1830s, but, like most folks around New Orleans then and now, he wasn't above a bit of moonlighting. In the evenings his drugstore became a semiofficial saloon for his friends, a place for him to experiment with spirits and medicines—though the line between the two in those days was a fine one.

As part of his ongoing lab project, Peychaud created a style of bitters for use in drinks that is sold under his name to this day. But, more important, he started mixing up brandy, absinthe, and a dash of those bitters to produce a high-octane concoction he served in an eggcup. Although this vessel was known in French as a *coquetier*, the pronunciation proved too much for the non-French who played a greater and greater role in the city's business and social life, and so *coquetier* evolved into "cocktay" and at last into "cocktail."

Once it had taken on a pronounceable American name, that "medicinally mixed" drink became America's very first cocktail. Yet its story wasn't finished yet. During the prosperous pre–Civil War period, Peychaud's basic recipe was adopted throughout the bars of New Orleans—and, between rich people drinking to remember and poor people drinking to forget, that meant a *lot* of bars. Each mixologist paid homage to Peychaud's original but also added twists, shakes, and splashes of his own. It was in 1853 that Sewell Taylor established the recipe for all time, using as his main ingredient a French brandy he imported and sold exclusively. That brandy was Sazerac de Forge et Fils, so the cocktail became known as the Sazerac. Taylor's establishment on Exchange Alley thus became known as the Sazerac Coffee House.

As irrefutable evidence that an *American* vision was slowly transforming once-French New Orleans, especially in the austerity that followed the South's defeat in the Civil War, the Sazerac became more about a company than a drink or even a coffeehouse. A man named Thomas Handy bought the coffeehouse in 1870, at the same time that he began to acquire and market various brands of liquor. He took on Peychaud's famous bitters at the start, later adding the Sazerac cocktail (by now made with whiskey rather than brandy) to his list of good stuff in a bottle. Handy's firm soon operated a new Sazerac Bar on Royal Street, the precursor of the one in the old Roosevelt Hotel across Canal Street. And finally, Handy's former secretary, C. J. O'Reilly, chartered today's Sazerac Company, an entity that guards the magic name from abuse with considerable devotion.

Comfort and Joy

New Orleans's formative years as a hard-drinking town, based on its booze-tolerant European roots and built upon its rough-and-tumble decades as a thriving port city, involved visionaries like M. W. Heron and the Ramos brothers. Ole Martin Wilkes was a bartender in the French Quarter in the 1870s when he began pondering a simple problem. Day in and day out, what Heron served most frequently was whiskey, a far cry from the small-batch bourbons and single-malt Scotches that drinkers revere in our day. This wildly inconsistent whiskey was distilled in Kentucky and Tennessee (for high proof far more than for flavor), then shipped by riverboat or barge south to New Orleans. The problem was that one never knew what the whiskey was going to taste like, either poured straight into a customer's glass or mixed into the ever-growing collection of cocktails.

Heron's soon-to-be-profitable solution was to blend the booze with a collection of local ingredients (lemon, lime, orange, and cherry) and a proprietary blend of spices and other flavorings (Moroccan cinnamon, Mexican vanilla, and beyond) to mask the inconsistency of the whiskey. The recipe, created in 1874, hit the market in 1889 as a response to a popular competitor of the day, Hats and Tails. Naming his concoction after other pieces of male plumage, Heron dubbed it Cuffs and Buttons.

His early successes with the liqueur, marketed under his name and with the claim "None Genuine but Mine" written on every bottle, propelled

Heron to the 1904 World's Fair in St. Louis, often described as the United States' first food festival because it introduced many new culinary inventions such as hot dogs and hamburgers. In addition to hitting it off with a true kindred "spirit," some guy named Jack Daniel from a dry county in Tennessee, Heron earned a gold medal at the fair for his product's quality and taste. Its secret recipe guarded more closely now than ever, Southern Comfort was born.

The Ramos brothers made their own mark on the alcoholic history of New Orleans in the early twentieth century, giving the world a cocktail that, though it's not known to many bartenders today, was all the rage for more than a decade. The brothers' cocktail, the Ramos gin fizz, went underground with most other worthwhile things during Prohibition (1920–33), but it reemerged, accompanied by the one surviving brother, Henry, to take its place in the 1930s in the often-tawdry, semi-bright lights of Louisiana politics.

The gin fizz created by the bartending brothers at their Imperial Cabinet Saloon seems a throwback to us now. Unlike the colorful concoctions we tend to order now, many with overly cute and suggestive names, the Ramos gin fizz was and is a class act. The gin in this drink goes uptown with the careful addition of cream and egg whites, and it goes exotic with hints of lemon, lime, and even orange flower water. The key ingredient, however, is hard work: the drink is meant to be shaken by the bartender somewhere between eight and forty times. That's the fizz!

According to local historians, the Ramos gin fizz, and by association the Ramos brothers, enjoyed their finest hours during the Carnival season of 1915. Demand at and around the Imperial Cabinet Saloon forced them to employ no fewer than thirty-five bartenders, who did little else for the costumed revelers than shake up gin fizz after gin fizz. Even then, the story goes, there was a line around the block.

Prohibition, which began in the hearts and minds of some soon after the Civil War, is often said to have affected New Orleans little even after it became official with the Volstead Act. That boast, of course, is hardly true. Alcohol may have continued to flow here, as it did in any rural area where people could erect stills and in any city where there was organized crime, but liquor makers and drinkers alike faced a struggle. It would be a different drama with a different cast of characters when the United States realized its mistake and repealed Prohibition with the 21st Amendment on December 5, 1933.

The one surviving Ramos brother, Henry, felt his future looked brighter not reopening the Imperial Cabinet but rather hooking up with a hotel, whose bar would later become famous for serving Antoine Peychaud's Sazerac. The Roosevelt seemed quite pleased to purchase both the recipe and the right to the Ramos name from Henry, setting dozens upon dozens of the frothy things before its well-heeled patrons each night. One of those patrons was Huey P. Long, a populist poor boy who became governor, then U.S. senator, and finally cast his eye on the White House before an assassin's bullet brought him down. Huey—as he is still known in Louisiana—loved the Roosevelt Hotel to distraction. They say he built a new highway from Baton Rouge to New Orleans so he could cover the 80-plus miles to the hotel bar a little faster.

History tells us the Ramos gin fizz was Huey's favorite drink in New Orleans, and once his ambitions carried him to the Senate in Washington, Huey knew one of the most important things he had to pack: one of the bartenders from the Roosevelt. In turn, that bartender taught others all over the nation's capital the secret to the drink.

Cocktail Heroes

Decades before planeloads of tourists began making their way to New Orleans to indulge in the city's food and drink, there was a profound link between serving stiff drinks and serving glorious meals. For the moment, overlook the fabled prominence of the Mafia in this city's political and social life—along with the mob invitation to "go eat spaghetti." What you realize is that it was booze that bankrolled the city's famed restaurant dynasties.

Take the story of Arnaud Cazenave, for example. Cazenave grew up a Frenchman of moderate means in the village of Pau. Somehow, he convinced his parents that he should go to America, attend medical school, and make his fortune as a doctor. Young Cazenave came to America and sought his fortune, but instead of studying to be a physician he became the next best thing—a liquor salesman. Cazenave's success as a liquor salesman, first in New York but increasingly in New Orleans, led him to purchase a bar on Bourbon Street. Patrons loved his drinks, his gracious hospitality, and the food he set out for free, and soon the idea formed in his mind that perhaps the food shouldn't be free anymore.

Cazenave opened Arnaud's, a smallish space on Bienville Street, in 1918, and year after year he expanded, until he occupied the entire city block. As the story goes, virtually all the buildings surrounding his were brothels—though that can probably be said of every building in the French Quarter, with the possible exception of St. Louis Cathedral. As each

madam quit the business or passed on to her final reward, Cazenave purchased her building. One challenge arose during Prohibition, when Cazenave was accused of selling liquor illegally and brought to trial. A local jury acquitted him, however, at least in part because by then he was well known around New Orleans as the Count. The Count—waking in his mansion on Esplanade to a bottle of champagne each morning and smoking cigars in his dining rooms each night—rose from liquor salesman to international culinary legend by the time of his death.

Owen Brennan worked as a liquor salesman as well. In fact, since he was both Irish and Catholic and was raising a large number of children, he might have forever remained a liquor salesman, unwilling to take the risk necessary to get into the restaurant business. But, according to one of those stories that no one can confirm or deny, one of his best customers—the French restaurateur Arnaud Cazenave—played a central role in encouraging Brennan to take a leap of faith.

Perhaps a master of motivational speaking before there was such a thing, or maybe just sick of all Brennan's wannabe whining, the Count mounted a campaign based on goading Brennan with the words, "What the hell does an Irishman know about French food?" When Owen Brennan had had it up to here from the Count, he opened a place on Bourbon Street called Brennan's and described it defiantly as a French restaurant. A schmoozer who might well have been the Count's equal, Brennan built his own food and drink dynasty, eventually moving Brennan's into new, larger digs on Royal Street before his unexpected death.

Looking back, it's hard to deny that all of Brennan's Irish-Catholic procreation proved a blessing in disguise. In the decades that followed his death, his restaurant would be run first by his siblings, then by his three sons, and now increasingly by their children. You need not weep for those siblings, though. They quickly took on Commander's Palace in the Garden District, not only training and inspiring chefs like Cajun genius Paul Prudhomme and some kid from Fall River, Massachusetts, named Emeril Lagasse, but also helping their own kids expand the Brennan dynasty in New Orleans, Las Vegas, and Disney-dazed Anaheim, California.

BAR STUFF

New Orleanians look upon the recent spate of cool equipment available for the home bartender with mixed emotions. Of course, it's always cool to own the latest gadgets, but it's the rare New Orleans family that doesn't have at least one uncle who's a bartender somewhere, ever ready to "borrow" something from work when the need arises. Also, there's the New Orleanians' talent for getting by on little or nothing, just like their ancestors did, and most in the Crescent City would agree they don't need a bunch of doohickeys just to make themselves a drink!

For all that, the newcomer to home bartending these days surely has more in mind than simply getting alcohol into some vessel from which it can be sipped, slurped, or slugged. He or she wants to create both classic cocktails (which often rely more on skill than stuff) and the newest, trendiest drinks (which usually rely more on stuff than skill). We trust that readers will find a happy medium between breaking the bank for every gadget imaginable and attempting to make do with nothing.

Glassware

Culinary shops are filled with specialty glasses these days, and it's easy to customize your glassware according to what you, your family, and your friends like to drink. The most versatile glass for your bar is the cocktail glass, which today is perhaps better known as a martini glass. Used not only for martinis but for a bevy of alcoholic beverages, the cocktail glass should almost always be chilled. Right up there with the cocktail glass in popularity is the margarita glass, which is a similar shape but bigger and rounder. For cognacs and most other liqueurs meant for sipping, graceful snifters are good to keep around. Most are formed to fit snugly in your cupped hand, allowing your palm to warm the liquid inside and release its honeylike aromas. Flutes (the long, tall glasses associated with weddings) and tulips (the same idea with a more graceful curve) are the two kinds of glassware most associated with one of the classiest drinks going. That category includes true champagne (from the Champagne region of France),

sparkling wine ("champagne" from anywhere other than the Champagne region of France), and the host of champagne cocktails that are so nice to sip when the heavier stuff just won't do. Tumblers are flat-bottomed, generally plain-looking glasses that come in all shapes and sizes. The most commonly used tumblers are the slender 8-ounce highball glass, the even more slender 10-ounce Collins glass (as in Tom), and the shorter, squatter Oliver Hardy to both these Stan Laurels, the old-fashioned glass, sometimes known as a "rocks" glass. Two additional glasses can round out your New Orleans bar collection: any of the available sizes of Gibraltar glasses (the style with the paneled design on the bottom two-thirds) and, if you really want to re-create Bourbon Street, the tall, curvaceous glass that looks like a hurricane lantern for serving, you guessed it, the Hurricane created at

Pat O'Brien's. For the beer drinkers in your crowd, two types of glasses are probably enough. For lagers and most other see-through beers, use a straight glass called a pilsner glass, named after Pilsen, the legendary Czech beer city. If you prefer more sludgy brews, check out the traditional English pint glass. For those who love coffee-based cocktails such as Irish coffee, there is also a special glass—a skinny, glass mug with a stem. And no, you don't have to be Irish to use it!

Cocktail Shakers

Can you think of any other accessory that will make you feel more like a bartender at the classic Sazerac Bar at the Fairmont Hotel? The market is now loaded with cocktail shakers, from ornamental to plain, large to small, expensive to cheap. To settle upon one, simply decide how much you care how it looks, how much liquid you want to shake, and how much you want to pay. Remember that, unlike blenders, cocktail shakers traditionally turn out one drink at a time. To turn your shaker into a cocktail factory is to deny yourself one of the greatest pleasures of mixing a drink from New Orleans: the feeling of tradition.

Blenders

Wimpy little countertop blenders beware! Bar blending is not for the faint of heart, the dull of blade, or the motor tending to overheat. Cocktails that benefit from a whirl in the blender require that your blender be able to turn ice cubes into some form of colorful slush. When choosing a blender, look for words like "professional" and "industrial." There are some nifty special effects being added to blenders these days, and there's nothing wrong with that, but if you select a blender for your home bar on any basis other than its power and its warranty, you're begging to have your cocktail party go up in smoke—perhaps literally.

Bar Tools

As any New Orleanian will tell you, you don't really need anything except a bottle of alcohol to make a drink, but any one of the sets of bar tools currently for sale in most housewares stores will make the whole process a lot more fun. A jigger is a super start to any set of bar tools, because measuring the ingredients will make any set of drink instructions feel more like a real recipe. Other great accoutrements include a winged corkscrew, a bar knife and spoon, a bottle opener, and a strainer that fits over the top of your shaker or your favorite size of cocktail glass. The hardcore might even throw in a zester, a whisk, and attractive ice tongs.

Bar Towels

Don't laugh—towels are part of the cocktail tradition, too. In fact, in movies and on TV, what do we mostly see bartenders doing? Wiping up their bar, of course. Plain white towels work just fine: they clean up nicely and aren't too expensive to replace when they get stained. Microfiber towels work especially well for polishing and repolishing your glassware—another act that makes you feel like a total professional.

Simple Syrup

These days, when so many popular cocktails are driven by significant amounts of sweetness, you must wonder how so much sugar gets into your glass. The answer: simple syrup. Simply (the name's not lying) dissolve 2 cups of sugar in 1 cup of water and boil for 5 minutes. Let the mixture cool and store it in a sealed jar in your refrigerator.

Big Easy
Drinks

{signatures}

In recent years, the cocktail has reemerged from perhaps two decades of playing sidekick to wine and even beer. In New Orleans, however, the cocktail never really went away, especially the kind of signature drinks that fathers offer to sons as a rite of passage. These famous cocktails of New Orleans tend to be traditional spirits put through the wringer of traditional technique, preferably by a bartender old enough to have been around when the drink was invented. Please pay attention to the ingredients, the tricky little procedures, and, yes, even the glasses used in these preparations. New Orleans drinkers understand that the act of making these cocktails is part religious ritual and part high theater. The devil, they know, is in the details.

Hurricane

Associated with both Pat O'Brien's, one of New Orleans's great bars, and the city's fabled party animal image, this drink packs a punch that is belied by its easy-to-drink flavor. Speaking of punch, if you miss the neon red of Hawaiian Punch, just add 1/2 ounce of grenadine to this real juice version.

1 1/2 ounces cranberry juice

1 1/4 ounces freshly squeezed orange juice

1 1/4 ounces pineapple juice

3/4 ounce sour mix

1/2 ounce Bacardi Light rum

1/2 ounce Bacardi Limón or any citrus-flavored rum

1/2 ounce Bacardi Select

1/2 ounce spiced rum

1/4 ounce Bacardi 151

1 maraschino cherry, for garnish

1 orange slice, for garnish

Combine all the ingredients except the cherry and orange slice and shake with ice. Strain into a Hurricane glass and garnish with the cherry and orange slice.

Recommended Listening:
Little Richard, "Tutti Frutti"

Sazerac

This first-ever cocktail was created by apothecary Antoine Peychaud him-self, before the recipe made the move across Canal Street to the legendary Roosevelt Hotel, now the Fairmont. Even today, the hotel and its glorious bar (with Paul Ninas's WPA murals of New Orleans life from the 1930s) have to pay legal homage to the Sazerac Co., which owns and closely controls rights to the recipe and, whenever it feels like it, the name. Misusing the word *Sazerac* is on a par locally with misusing the name or image of that mouse who lives in Orlando.

Pernod, for coating glass

1¼ ounces rye whiskey

2 dashes Peychaud bitters

1 sugar cube

Pour a small amount of Pernod into an old-fashioned glass, swirl to coat the glass, then pour out any excess. Combine the rye whiskey, bitters, and sugar cube and shake with ice. Strain into the prepared glass.

Recommended Listening: Harry Connick Jr., "It's All Right with Me"

SIGNATURES

Ramos Gin Fizz

There are gin fizzes in this world—and then there's the frothy one perfected by Henry Ramos at the old Roosevelt Hotel. Louisiana governor Huey "Kingfish" Long loved the drink so much that he imported the recipe to Washington when he moved there to serve in the U.S. Senate. "Ole Huey," as he is still known around his favorite hotel, was gunned down in the corridors of the Louisiana State Capitol Building during a heated legislative session, but his beloved Ramos gin fizz lives on.

> **3 ounces soda water**
>
> **2 ounces milk**
>
> **1¼ ounces simple syrup (page 15)**
>
> **1½ ounces gin**
>
> **½ ounce freshly squeezed lime juice**
>
> **1 egg white**
>
> **2 drops orange flower water**

Combine all the ingredients and shake with ice until the egg white is frothy. Strain into an old-fashioned glass filled with fresh ice.

♕ **Recommended Listening:** Neville Brothers, "If It Takes All Night"

Brandy Milk Punch

As a hard-drinking town with a serious affection for late-night carousing, New Orleans has developed or adopted more than its fair share of what locals optimistically describe as "eye-openers" (basically, that's shorthand for a hangover cure, also known as the hair of the dog). Something this milky and frothy is bound to soothe a protesting morning-after stomach.

2 ounces half-and-half

2 ounces milk

1 1/2 ounces brandy

1 tablespoon simple syrup (page 15)

6 drops vanilla extract

Ground nutmeg, for dusting

Combine all the ingredients except the nutmeg and shake with ice. Strain into a chilled highball glass with a little fresh ice. Dust with nutmeg.

Recommended Listening: Irma Thomas, "It's Raining"

Mint Julep

Once upon a time New Orleanians dismissed this summer refreshment as part of the old South that only existed in *Gone with the Wind*. In other words, they saw mint juleps as part of that half-remembered, half-made-up glorious past on all those Dixie plantations. Eventually, though, the flavor of the julep won over all but the staunchest traditionalists. If more New Orleanians had verandas, they'd drink even more mint juleps.

1$^{1}/_{4}$ ounces bourbon

1 lime, quartered

1 sugar cube

4 leaves fresh mint

Soda water

Mint sprig, for garnish

Combine the bourbon, lime quarters, sugar cube, and mint leaves in a Collins glass. Top with crushed ice and soda water and gently stir. Garnish with the mint sprig and serve.

Recommended Listening: Allen Toussaint, "Southern Nights"

French 75

Some folks like any drink named after something that explodes or mows people down. Decades before the Hand Grenade became a favorite on and off Bourbon Street, Count Arnaud Cazenave of Arnaud's laid claim to inventing the French 75. Although some claim the drink originated in New York or Paris, no one doubts the drink was named after the French 75-millimeter cannon used effectively on the Western Front during World War I.

1 ounce brandy

$1/2$ ounce freshly squeezed lemon juice

$1/4$ ounce simple syrup (page 15)

Champagne

Combine the brandy, lemon juice, and simple syrup and shake with ice. Strain into a champagne glass filled with fresh ice and top with champagne.

Recommended Listening: Ivory Joe Hunter, "Jumpin' at the Dew Drop"

Absinthe Suissese

Nothing speaks as directly to the heart of New Orleans drinking as absinthe does. Before its banishment as a dangerous substance in the early years of the twentieth century—against the same cultural background that pushed Prohibition down America's throat—the licorice-flavored spirit was incredibly popular. Associated with painters, poets, and others likely to go off the deep end anyway, absinthe often took the rap for their erratic behavior. There are some in the United States, France, and elsewhere who want real absinthe returned to the drink menu—especially for cocktails like this French Quarter classic.

SIGNATURES

1 ounce absinthe substitute

1 ounce egg white

^{1}/4 ounce anisette

^{1}/2 ounce green crème de menthe

1 dash orange flower water

Coarse sugar

Mint sprig, for garnish

Combine all the ingredients except the coarse sugar and mint sprig and shake until the egg white is frothy. Strain into a champagne glass with a sugared rim. Garnish with the mint sprig and serve.

♔ Recommended Listening:
Aaron Neville, "Tell It Like It Is"

Mimosa

This is the brunch beverage extraordinaire. And since the "second breakfasts" enjoyed by workers in the French Market a century ago are considered the origin and inspiration for the brunch served today, why shouldn't this marriage of bubbles and vitamin C get the nod all over town as morning fades gracefully into afternoon?

2 ounces freshly squeezed orange juice

4 ounces champagne

Pour the orange juice into a champagne flute and top with the champagne.

♛ Recommended Listening: Fats Domino, "Walkin' to New Orleans"

SIGNATURES

Pimm's Royale

This champagne cocktail shares much of the same history as the Pimm's Cup, drawing its spirit (literally and figuratively) from the creation of James Pimm in his London oyster bar. This drink, however, is even simpler, replacing the lemonade and soda water with the champagne of your choice.

3/4 ounce Pimm's No. 1

Champagne

1 lemon twist, for garnish

Pour the Pimm's into a champagne glass and fill with champagne. Garnish with the lemon twist.

♛ Recommended Listening: Aaron Neville, "Mona Lisa"

Pimm's Cup

Perhaps because the city has long been associated with all things French, New Orleanians don't typically engage in activities even remotely associated with Great Britain. Still, this drink created by James Pimm at his London oyster bar in the 1840s has come to find a sizable fan club in the Crescent City. Not atypically, most New Orleanians figure it was invented here.

> **2 ounces Pimm's No. 1**
>
> **3 ounces fresh lemonade (page 77)**
>
> **Soda water**
>
> **1 cucumber slice, for garnish**

Pour the Pimm's into an old-fashioned glass over ice and add the lemonade. Add just a dash of soda water. Stir and garnish with the cucumber slice.

Recommended Listening: Lil' Queenie, "My Darlin' New Orleans"

Bloody Mary

Naturally enjoyed as a morning beverage, the Bloody Mary was predestined to be embraced by hungover New Orleanians as yet another "eye-opener." Like many New Orleans indulgences, this drink incorporates something that's healthy for you—in this case, tomato juice—allowing those who enjoy it to declare debauchery good for you.

4 ounces V8 juice

$1^{1}/_{4}$ ounces vodka

$^{3}/_{4}$ teaspoon prepared horseradish

$^{1}/_{2}$ teaspoon celery salt

$^{1}/_{2}$ teaspoon black pepper

**1 dash Sriracha Hot Chili Sauce or
  other hot pepper sauce**

2 olives, for garnish

1 lime wedge, for garnish

1 celery stick, for garnish

Combine the V8 juice, vodka, horseradish, celery salt, pepper, and chile sauce and shake with ice. Strain into a Collins glass with fresh ice and garnish with the olives, lime wedge, and celery stick.

Recommended Listening: Huey "Piano" Smith, "Don't You Just Know It"

Pousse Café

No, you won't find a Pousse Café on most modern New Orleans bar menus—or indeed even someone capable of making the layered drink behind most modern New Orleans bars—but you *will* find the drink mentioned lovingly in many literary works from New Orleans in the late nineteenth century. The original version, supposedly created by a local saloon owner named Joseph Santina, was somewhat different, we're told, but the version made today consists of several layers of colorful liqueurs. Don't be intimidated: a moderate amount of care produces a dazzling result.

¹/₄ ounce grenadine

¹/₄ ounce crème de cacao

¹/₄ ounce cherry liqueur

¹/₄ ounce orange curaçao

¹/₄ ounce green crème de menthe

¹/₂ ounce cognac

Carefully pour each ingredient in the order listed over the back of a spoon, letting them slowly slide into a Pousse Café or any medium-size, clear glass to form distinct layers. Do not stir before serving.

👑 Recommended Listening:
Smiley Lewis, "Blue Monday"

Bloody Bull

Just about everybody agrees the Bloody Mary was created at the Ritz Bar in Paris right after World War I, conveniently coinciding with the first shipment of tomato juice from the United States. Similarly, this reverse import—basically a Bloody Mary with beef broth added—sprang up in the United States in the 1960s, when vodka first started showing up in American liquor cabinets. With both tomato juice and beef broth, it's even better for you, we say.

> **3 ounces beef broth**
>
> **2 ounces V8 juice**
>
> **1 1/2 ounces vodka**
>
> **1/8 teaspoon black pepper**
>
> **4 dashes hot pepper sauce**
>
> **1 dash freshly squeezed orange juice**
>
> **1 thinly sliced orange peel, for garnish**

Combine all the ingredients except the orange peel and shake well. Pour into a tumbler or Collins glass over fresh ice. Garnish with the orange peel.

♔ Recommended Listening: The Spiders, "I Didn't Want to Do It"

Just like New Orleans cuisine, cocktails in the Big Easy are a living, evolving art. You might not think so visiting some of the older saloons in the city, but it's true. The result is what we call the "new classics," cocktails that are rooted in tradition, linked to New Orleans's history in some way, even though they weren't served in the city's past. These cocktails, served nightly (and even daily) at the Heaven on Seven restaurants, capture the true spirit and flair of the Creole and Cajun people of south Louisiana that we love so much, while perhaps showing them a taste or two they haven't tried yet. We trust that you'll enjoy these new classics every bit as much as we and our guests do.

{new classics}

Crawdaddy

At Heaven on Seven, bartenders have long enjoyed preparing guests for their first encounter with bright-red spicy boiled crawfish with a drink that features the same color scheme. The crawfish, also known as crawdads or less appealingly as "mud bugs," come piping hot in a mammoth pile arranged on a table covered with sheets of newspaper.

4 ounces lemonade

$1^1/_4$ ounces Bacardi Limón or any citrus-flavored rum

1 ounce cranberry juice

1 lemon wedge, for garnish

Pour the lemonade, rum, and cranberry juice over crushed ice in a 22-ounce glass—a Gibraltar glass if you have one. Stir and garnish with the lemon wedge.

Recommended Listening: Huey Smith, "Rockin' Pneumonia"

Bayou Punch

Everybody's home bartending bag of tricks could use a punch like this one Heaven on Seven named after the Bayou Country outside New Orleans. Needless to say, its refreshing, citrusy flavor makes it go down real easy when the weather is hot. Or whatever the weather is. For the uninitiated, Green River Soda is a slightly sweet, lime-flavored, and very bright-green colored soda that's been a favorite in the Midwest for nearly 100 years.

4 ounces lemonade

1¹/₄ ounces Bacardi Limón or any citrus-flavored rum

1 ounce Green River Soda

1 lemon wedge, for garnish

Pour the lemonade, rum, and soda over crushed ice in a 22-ounce glass— a Gibraltar glass if you have one. Stir and garnish with the lemon wedge.

♔ Recommended Listening: The Radiators, "Sunglasses On"

Southern Comfort Eggnog

Southern Comfort is a liqueur created in New Orleans by a bartender named M. W. Heron. Originally sold as Cuffs and Buttons (a reference to the classy white tie and tails), it became Southern Comfort sometime after Heron transferred his base of operations to St. Louis. Though it turns up regularly around New Orleans in holiday eggnog recipes like this one, it's also hard for men and women of a certain age to forget the image of Janis Joplin swigging the stuff onstage.

6 large eggs

1/2 cup sugar

3/4 cup Southern Comfort

4 cups heavy cream

Vanilla extract

Ground nutmeg, for dusting

Separate the egg yolks from the whites into separate bowls. Lightly beat the sugar with the yolks, then incorporate the Southern Comfort. Refrigerate the yolk mixture and the egg whites separately overnight. When ready to serve, whip the cream until soft peaks form and fold it into the yolk mixture. In a clean bowl, whip the egg whites until stiff peaks form and fold into the cream mixture. Add vanilla to taste and stir. Pour into a punch bowl and dust with nutmeg. Serves 8 to 10.

Recommended Listening: Smiley Lewis, "Bells Are Ringing"

Gentilly Sunrise

Gentilly is one of the older New Orleans residential areas—a place many older locals remember fondly, even if the visitors who bebop from the French Quarter to the Garden District seldom make their way there. The "sunrise" here refers to the swirl of bright-red grenadine.

3 ounces freshly squeezed orange juice

1¹/₄ ounces Bacardi Light rum

1 splash grenadine

1 orange slice, for garnish

1 maraschino cherry, for garnish

Combine the lemon juice and rum and shake with ice. Strain into a Collins glass with fresh ice. Top the drink with a splash of grenadine and garnish with the orange slice and cherry.

Recommended Listening:
Benny Spellman, "Fortune Teller"

Cakewalk into Town

Chocolate, vanilla and a touch of raspberry make a wonderful cake for dessert. But in this class-act rendition, we prove they can join forces to become a wonderful cocktail as well. Perfect for those who want to have their dessert and *drink* it too!

1 ounce vanilla-flavored vodka

1 ounce Godiva dark chocolate liqueur

$^3/_4$ ounce Chambord

$1^1/_4$ ounces half-and-half

1 cherry, for garnish

Pour the vodka, chocolate liqueur, Chambord, and half-and-half into a mixing glass with ice. Shake and strain into a chilled martini glass. Garnish with the cherry.

♛ **Recommended Listening:** Taj Mahal, "Cakewalk into Town"

Cajun Iced Tea

Drink your heart out, Manhattan. Just like you, the people of the Bayou Country of south Louisiana have their own high-octane version of the Deep South's favorite summer beverage. This one delivers a three-liquor punch that'll make you ask, right along with New Orleans legend Allen Toussaint, "Have you ever seen those Southern nights?"

1 1/2 ounces sour mix

1 1/4 ounces Bacardi Limón or any citrus-flavored rum

1 1/4 ounces Kahlúa

1 1/4 ounces premium tequila

1 ounce cranberry juice

1 lemon slice, for garnish

1 cucumber slice, for garnish

Lemon leaves, for garnish

Pour all the ingredients except the lemon slice over crushed ice in a 22-ounce glass—preferably a Gibraltar glass if you have one. Stir and garnish with the lemon slice, cucumber slice, and lemon leaves.

♔ Recommended Listening: Louis Armstrong with Earl "Fatha" Hines, "Basin Street Blues"

NEW CLASSICS

Piña Po-Lada

In the famous local food word *po-boy* (as in sandwich), the word *po* is obviously jargon for "poor." But we think you'll agree there's absolutely nothing poor about this new spun variation on one of the Caribbean's most popular drinks, the piña colada—except maybe for the fact that it doesn't require a blender, in case (poor) you don't have one. Besides, with just a little half-and-half subbing for that hyper-fattening coconut cream, you can drink lots more of them.

> **1½ ounces Bacardi Light rum**
>
> **1 ounce Malibu rum**
>
> **2 ounces pineapple juice**
>
> **½ ounce half-and-half**
>
> **1 pineapple slice, for garnish**

Pour the light rum, Malibu rum, pineapple juice, and half-and-half into a mixing glass with ice. Shake and strain into a tall rocks glass filled with ice. Garnish with the pineapple slice.

♚ **Recommended Listening:** Jimmy Buffet, "I Will Play for Gumbo"

During America's great cocktail renaissance, no drink has enjoyed more of a rediscovery than the martini. Long associated with both classic American characters (can anyone forget Nick and Nora Charles in the Thin Man movies, solving murders between shakers full of the clear cocktail) and the quintessential Brit James Bond, the martini has always had an impressive pedigree. What it didn't have for way too long was a hip attitude. With Jimmy's Big-Ass Martinis, we take the martini down off its pedestal and reinvent it in several fun ways best enjoyed in the company of friends, lovers, and, hopefully, at least a few designated drivers.

{jimmy's big-ass martinis}

Jimmy's Love Potion

The idea of a "love potion" has a powerful hold on New Orleanians. After all, one of the concoctions that Marie Laveau and her voodoo peers were most often asked to whip up was one that would make somebody fall madly in love with somebody else. This recipe may have the same effect—and it's certain to make anybody look more appealing at least until morning.

3 ounces Bacardi Limón or any citrus-flavored rum

¼ ounce Cointreau

1 splash Rose's lime juice

1 splash cranberry juice

1 lemon twist, for garnish

Combine the rum, Cointreau, Rose's lime juice, and cranberry juice and shake with ice. Strain into a cocktail glass and garnish with the lemon twist.

♛ Recommended Listening: Earl King, "Those Lonely, Lonely Nights"

Cajun Martini

Beginning in the 1980s, America started associating any peppery food or drink with the Cajuns. Real Cajuns weren't really happy with this state of affairs, since their foods and drinks are distinguished by their wonderful flavors rather than just their heat. All that, however, didn't keep a gumbo pot of Cajun chefs from experimenting with pepper-infused vodkas. To make your very own supply of pepper-infused vodka, insert 2 habenero peppers, seeded or not depending on your thirst for heat, into a bottle of vodka at least one day in advance of using.

3 ounces habanero-infused vodka

$1/4$ ounce vodka

1 cherry pepper, for garnish

Combine the vodkas and shake with ice. Strain into a cocktail glass and garnish with the cherry pepper.

Recommended Listening:
Bobby Charles, "See You Later, Alligator"

Lucky Seven

A visit to the casino on the Mississippi River has become a regular event for New Orleans locals and visitors alike, and some of them might want to take a gamble on this fruity martini variation. Creoles and Cajuns have always bet the rent money on anything that moved. A dice game here in the nineteenth century was called *les crapauds* (the frogs) by a wealthy bon vivant named Bernard de Marigny de Mandeville. Since his American gambling buddies couldn't quite pronounce the name, they shortened it to "craps." Just for the record, old Bernard died pretty much destitute.

> **3 ounces premium vodka**
>
> **1³/₄ ounces peach schnapps**
>
> **³/₄ ounce freshly squeezed orange juice**
>
> **¹/₄ ounce cranberry juice**
>
> **1 peach slice, for garnish**

Combine the vodka, schnapps, orange juice, and cranberry juice and shake with ice. Strain into a cocktail glass and garnish with the peach slice.

♛ Recommended Listening: Shirley Goodman and Leonard Lee, "Let the Good Times Roll"

Southern Limeade

As those who enjoy drinking a margarita or a mojito on a hot day know, there just isn't anything much more refreshing than lime juice. This drink sticks close to your basic limeade recipe, except, of course, it's got a kick of vodka for the grown-ups.

> **3 ounces vodka**
>
> **³/4 ounce freshly squeezed lime juice**
>
> **³/4 ounce simple syrup (page 15)**
>
> **1 dash of Rose's lime juice**
>
> **1 lime wedge, for garnish**

Combine the vodka, fresh lime juice, simple syrup, and Rose's lime juice and shake with ice. Strain into a martini glass and garnish with the lime wedge.

Recommended Listening: Joe Banashak, "I Like It Like That"

Mardi Gras Martini

This is the sort of classy concoction you might not associate with the bedlam of Mardi Gras, but that's only because you've never scored an invite to any of the mansions along St. Charles Avenue on Fat Tuesday itself.

3 ounces lemon-flavored vodka

$^3/_4$ ounces Chambord

1 lemon twist, for garnish

Combine the vodka and Chambord and shake with ice. Strain into a cocktail glass and garnish with the lemon twist.

♛ Recommended Listening: Dr. John, "All on a Mardi Gras Day"

Nutty Professor Martini

It was Jerry Lewis who played the nutty professor in the movie of that name, but it's liqueurs made with walnut and hazelnut that star in this big-screen drink. Plus, the Godiva contribution mixes with half-and-half to make this a cocktail that goes down easily.

1 ounce Nocello walnut liqueur

1 ounce Frangelico hazelnut liqueur

$1^1/_2$ ounces Godiva dark chocolate liqueur

$^1/_2$ ounce half-and-half or cream

Combine all the ingredients and shake with ice. Strain into a chilled cocktail glass.

♛ Recommended Listening: Pete Fountain, "Walking through New Orleans"

Metrotini

Upon first hearing *metrosexual*, most men sat up and took notice, wondering how much they really liked to shop. After a few Metrotinis, however, even the least fashion-friendly male will happily submit to a pedicure.

> **1 ounce Absolute Mandarin vodka**
>
> **3/4 ounce Cointreau**
>
> **1 ounce cranberry juice**
>
> **1/2 ounce champagne**

Combine the vodka, Cointreau, and cranberry juice and shake with ice. Pour the champagne into a chilled martini glass, then strain the shaker contents over the champagne.

♕ Recommended Listening: Preservation Hall Jazz Band, "When the Saints Go Marching In"

Ginger Cosmo Martini

Besides a name that combines two of America's favorite cocktails, this creation weaves a certain ginger zing into the mix.

> **3 ounces ginger-flavored vodka**
>
> **1 1/2 ounces Cointreau**
>
> **3/4 ounce freshly squeezed lime juice**
>
> **1 1/2 ounces cranberry juice**

Combine all the ingredients and shake with ice. Strain into a chilled cocktail glass.

♕ Recommended Listening: Rockin' Dopsie Jr., "I'm the Zydeco Man"

Jack-O-Tini

Between the legions of fang-implanted pseudo-vampires on the trail of Anne Rice and the French Quarter's self-expressed gay population, Halloween in New Orleans has emerged as a celebration quite removed from the trick-or-treating we did as children. This orange cocktail recalls the color of a jack-o'-lantern.

2 ounces vanilla-flavored vodka

2 ounces freshly squeezed orange juice

1 splash lemon-lime soda

1 splash heavy cream

Combine all the ingredients and shake with ice. Strain into a cocktail glass.

Recommended Listening: Jessie Hill, "Ooo Poo Pah Do"

French Quarter Martini

New Orleans's French Quarter has embraced the modern martini right along with the rest of America. In fact, it's one of those trendy drinks that's been made and enjoyed behind the neighborhood's perennially closed shutters as long as anybody can remember. Then again, remembering is not always so easy after a few well-made martinis.

3 ounces lemon-flavored vodka

³/₄ ounce Chambord

³/₄ ounce pineapple juice

Lemon leaves, for garnish

1 lemon twist, for garnish

Combine the vodka, Chambord, and pineapple juice and shake with ice. Strain into a cocktail glass and garnish with the lemon leaves and a lemon twist.

👑 Recommended Listening:
Luther Kent, "Long, Long Day"

Mother Pucker Martini

This cocktail will definitely make you want to pucker up, whether for the kiss you'll surely want after a few or just from the pleasurable sting of the drink itself.

3 ounces premium vodka

1¹/₄ ounces Apple Pucker

1 splash sour mix

1 maraschino cherry, for garnish

Combine the vodka, Apple Pucker, and sour mix and shake with ice. Strain into a cocktail glass and garnish with the cherry.

♔ **Recommended Listening:** Ernie K-Doe, "Mother-in-Law"

"Lovely Rita" may have been one of the most hummable songs on the Beatles' album **Sgt. Pepper's Lonely Hearts Club Band,** but it's also apparently the theme song of a lot of folks sitting around the bar at Heaven on Seven. If the martini came back from the grave during the cocktail's rebirth in this country, the margarita came pretty much out of nowhere. At some point in the twentieth century, Mexican restaurants in Texas took to offering these bold, citrusy tequila drinks served with salt on the rim of each glass—yet the margarita remained in the Tex-Mex mode for decades. Finally, someone discovered that margaritas could not only serve as a sidekick to salsa but also incorporate almost any flavor you like. In this, the margarita resembles the martini, being less a hard-and-fast recipe than a versatile formula for creating all sorts of delicious drinks.

{ritas from heaven}

Ponchatoula Strawberry Rita

About an hour outside of New Orleans, Ponchatoula promotes itself most of the year as a terrific place to go antiquing. During the too-short summer season, however, everything in and around Ponchatoula is all about the strawberries. There's even a strawberry festival.

3 ounces sour mix

1 1/4 ounces premium tequila

3/4 ounce Grand Marnier

3/4 ounce fresh strawberry puree

Salt

1 lime wedge, for garnish

Combine the sour mix, tequila, Grand Marnier, and strawberry puree and shake with ice. Strain into a margarita glass with a salted rim filled with crushed ice. Garnish with the lime wedge.

♛ Recommended Listening: Oliver Morgan, "Who Shot the La-La"

Ragin' Cajun Rita

We've always loved the phrase "Ragin' Cajun." Not only is it the name of a Louisiana college sports team, but it also refers to some of the more colorful characters of Acadiana (even though we've generally found the people there to be both friendly and pleasantly laid-back—in other words, not ragin' at all!). This version of the margarita is one of the most popular drinks at Heaven on Seven.

3 ounces sour mix

1 1/4 ounces premium tequila

3/4 ounce Grand Marnier

3/4 ounce freshly squeezed orange juice

Salt

1 lime wedge, for garnish

Combine the sour mix, tequila, Grand Marnier, and orange juice and shake with ice. Strain into a margarita glass with a salted rim filled with crushed ice. Garnish with the lime wedge.

Recommended Listening: Sugarboy and the Cane Cutters, "I Don't Know What I'll Do"

Ruston Peach Rita

Yes, we know that peaches are traditionally associated with Georgia, but some of the very best we've ever tasted have come from Louisiana. The area around Ruston celebrates the fuzzy fruits each peach season, so of course we had to name our peach margarita in the town's honor.

3 ounces sour mix

1$^{1}/_{4}$ ounces premium tequila

$^{3}/_{4}$ ounce Grand Marnier

$^{3}/_{4}$ ounces fresh peach puree

Salt

1 lime wedge, for garnish

Combine the sour mix, tequila, Grand Marnier, and peach puree and shake with ice. Strain into a margarita glass with a salted rim filled with crushed ice. Garnish with the lime wedge.

👑 Recommended Listening: Johnny Adams, "Reconsider Me"

Blue Bayou Margarita

Roy Orbison and Linda Ronstadt should be so proud that the song they made their own inspired this margarita. The bright blue color comes, of course, from the liqueur called curaçao but the punch, make no mistake, comes from the tequila.

1 ounce premium tequila

1 ounce blue curaçao

2$^1/_2$ ounces sour mix

1 splash of Rose's lime juice

1 lime slice, for garnish

Combine the tequila, blue curacao, sour mix, and lime juice and shake with ice. Strain into a margarita glass with a salted rim filled with crushed ice. Garnish with the lime slice.

Recommended Listening: Pete Fountain, "Do You Know What It Means to Miss New Orleans"

Cranberry Margarita

Whatever you think of drinking the stuff straight, we believe cranberry juice is one of the great under-utilized ingredients in any bar. It adds the two things you need most in a cocktail, flavor and color, and it seems remarkably adaptable to different preparations and presentations. Not bad for something that comes from a bog!

1¹/₂ ounces premium tequilla

¹/₂ ounce Grand Marnier

3 ounces cranberry juice

1 splash of Rose's lime juice

1 lime slice, for garnish

Combine the tequila, Grand Marnier, cranberry juice, and lime juice and shake with ice. Strain into a margarita glass with a salted rim filled with crushed ice. Garnish with the slice of lime.

♕ Recommended Listening: Al Hirt, "Bourbon Street Parade"

Mardi Gras Mango Rita

By the time Ash Wednesday finally rolls around, all those celebrating the Carnival season leading up to Mardi Gras itself have heard the great song "Mardi Gras Mambo" approximately 3,539 times. Looking for a name for our popular mango margarita, we couldn't resist making the Carnival connection.

3 ounces sour mix

1 1/4 ounces premium tequila

3/4 ounce Grand Marnier

3/4 ounce fresh mango puree

Salt

1 lime slice, for garnish

Combine the sour mix, tequila, Grand Marnier, and mango puree and shake with ice. Strain into a margarita glass with a salted rim filled with crushed ice. Garnish with the lime slice.

♛ Recommended Listening:
The Hawkettes, "Mardi Gras Mambo"

Melon Margarita

Midori, besides being the name of a famous violinist from Japan, is one of the first melon-based liqueurs to grab up a faithful following in the United States. The green color can be quite lovely, whether in the bottle on your bar top or mixed into a cocktail such as this.

1¹/₂ ounces premium tequila

¹/₂ ounce Grand Marnier

1 ounce Midori melon liqueur

2 ounces sour mix

Salt

1 lime wedge, for garnish

Combine all the ingredients and shake with ice. Strain into a margarita glass with a salted rim filled with crushed ice. Garnish with the lime wedge.

Recommended Listening: The Wild Tchoupitoulas, "Big Chief Got a Golden Crown"

It's one of the great mysteries of modern existence: the more we become and, hopefully, act
like adults, the more we long for the consol-
ing tastes and textures of childhood. Any
New Orleans dessert chef understands this
well, dishing up warm pecan pie or peach
cobbler that most of us only pretend our
mothers used to make. Bartenders are doing
much the same thing when they take ice
cream and turn it into a soothing, comfort-
food cocktail.

The noble snowball, which those in some
other places have the nerve to call a snow
cone, is one of the elemental pleasures of New
Orleans life. In the summer, like toadstools
after a gentle rain, little shacks spring up on
nearly every street corner. Like so many
great things in New Orleans, snowballs are a
great equalizer, and corporate warlords in
Italian suits line up for this respite from the
heat beside the shirtless urchins next in line.

{frozen drinks}

Big Muddy

By the time it reaches New Orleans from someplace too far away to take seriously—someplace like Minnesota, we're told—the water of the Mississippi River that started out blue (a rumor, once again) has picked up enough of the American heartland to turn a muddy brown, thus the name of this wonderful ice cream drink.

2 scoops vanilla ice cream

1 ounce vanilla-flavored vodka

³/₄ ounce Patrón XO Café

³/₄ ounce Grand Marnier

Combine all the ingredients in a blender and blend until thick and smooth. Pour into a stemmed glass and serve with a straw.

Recommended Listening: Frankie Ford, "Sea Cruise"

Triple Chocolate

There's one in every crowd—and statistics tell us it's probably a she rather than a he—the chocolate lover. You know who you are.

2 scoops chocolate ice cream

1 ounce vodka

1 ounce Godiva dark chocolate liqueur

1 splash Vermeer chocolate liqueur

Combine all the ingredients in a blender and blend until thick and smooth. Pour into a stemmed glass and serve with a straw.

Recommended Listening: Benny Spellman, "Lipstick Traces"

Pralines and Cream

In the old days, the unforgettable brown sugar and pecan confections called pralines (that's PRAW-leens, never PRAY-leens) were sold on the streets by Creole women in bright bandanas called *tignons*. That was then, this is now. Not only are pralines still great to munch on as a sweet snack or dessert, but their elemental flavors of the South also make one heck of a drink.

2 scoops vanilla ice cream

1$^1/_4$ ounces vanilla-flavored vodka

$^1/_4$ ounce Nocello walnut liqueur

$^1/_4$ ounce Frangelico hazelnut liqueur

$^1/_4$ ounce amaretto

1 tablespoon chopped hazelnuts, for garnish

Combine the ice cream, vodka, liqueurs, and amaretto in a blender and blend until thick and smooth. Pour into a stemmed glass, garnish with the hazelnuts, and serve with a straw.

Recommended Listening:
The Dixie Cups, "Chapel of Love"

Naughty Girl Scout

If you're a scout leader, don't get all outraged about this drink's name. It's a tribute—honest. Surely you remember how hard it is to stop eating those peppermint-chocolate cookies. Well, if you love those cookies, you'll love this amazingly similar cocktail drink even more.

2 scoops vanilla ice cream

1³/₄ ounces Kahlúa

³/₄ ounce Rumpleminze or other peppermint schnapps

Combine all the ingredients in a blender and blend until thick and smooth. Pour into a stemmed glass and serve with a straw.

Recommended Listening: Guitar Slim, "The Things I Used to Do"

Bananas Foster

This drink goes boldly where no bartender has gone before, combining all the flavors of Owen Brennan's signature dessert—based on the ingredients he saw coming in through the port of New Orleans—into one luscious liquid.

2 scoops vanilla ice cream

1 peeled banana

³/₄ ounce Bacardi Select

¹/₄ ounce banana liqueur

¹/₈ teaspoon ground cinnamon

Combine all the ingredients in a blender and blend until thick and smooth. Pour into a stemmed glass and serve with a straw.

Recommended Listening: Professor Longhair, "Tipitina"

Cherries Jubilee

If you're having dinner at Antoine's in the French Quarter, you might forgo the flaming bananas Foster for something invented in-house, their *cerise jubilee*, cherries flamed with brandy and served with vanilla ice cream. Our version contains those same wonderful flavors poured over a New Orleans snowball.

1 ounce brandy

³/₄ ounce Peter Heering cherry liqueur

¹/₂ ounce orange curaçao

¹/₂ ounce freshly squeezed lemon juice

Combine all the ingredients and shake with ice. Strain over finely crushed or shaved ice in a Collins glass.

👑 Recommended Listening: Roy Brown, "Good Rockin' Tonight"

Key Lime Cream

Though snowballs were invented as refreshment for hot summer days, somewhere along the way cream sneaked into the picture. Maybe, since this is fat-loving New Orleans, that shouldn't surprise us much. Here we re-create in snowball form everybody's favorite flavor from the Florida Keys.

3 ounces heavy cream

2 ounces freshly squeezed key lime juice

1¹/₂ ounces gin

Combine all the ingredients and shake with ice. Strain over finely crushed or shaved ice in a Collins glass.

👑 Recommended Listening: Lee Dorsey, "Workin' in a Coal Mine"

Daiquiri

It didn't take long for the Caribbean's signature drink, the daiquiri (remember Hemingway downing drinks at the Floridita in Havana in those weird, wild days before Castro?) to make some headway in New Orleans. The weather is Caribbean enough, as is the culture. At the height of summer, when all the kids are begging for snowballs on the street, we grown-ups get to go inside, relax in the air-conditioning, and sip on a snowball of our own.

> **1 1/2 ounces white rum**
>
> **3/4 ounce simple syrup (page 15)**
>
> **3/4 ounce freshly squeezed lime juice**
>
> **1/2 ounce freshly squeezed grapefruit juice**
>
> **1/4 ounce maraschino liqueur**

Combine all the ingredients and shake with ice. Strain over finely crushed or shaved ice in a Collins glass.

♔ Recommended Listening: Dr. John, "Iko Iko"

Orange Orange

Trix are for kids, remember? Since three out of the four ingredients here feature the taste of oranges, we went ahead and named this snowball syrup after one of the flavors in that unavoidable breakfast cereal. And of course, crazy rabbit, these snowballs *aren't* for kids.

3 ounces freshly squeezed orange juice

3 ounces cranberry juice

1^1/$_2$ ounces orange-flavored vodka

1^1/$_2$ ounces Cointreau

3 cranberries, for garnish

1 orange twist, for garnish

Combine all the ingredients and shake with ice. Strain over finely crushed or shaved ice in a Collins glass. Garnish with the cranberries and orange twist.

♔ Recommended Listening: The Meters, "Hey Pocky Way"

Piña Colada

Do you like piña coladas, and gettin' caught in the rain? Whether or not you're old enough to remember that song, if you're over 21, you're old enough to enjoy this snowball. The key ingredient is the coconut cream—a glory not found in nature. Coconut cream was invented in Puerto Rico in the 1950s by a man named Don Ramon López-Irizarry. Don Ramon, we love you, man!

4 ounces pineapple juice

2 ounces Coco López coconut cream

1¹/₂ ounces light rum

1 ounce dark rum

1 ounce heavy cream

Combine all the ingredients and shake with ice. Strain over finely crushed or shaved ice in a Collins glass.

Recommended Listening: Robert Parker, "Barefootin'"

Long before Seattle parlayed its caffeine-rich Scandinavian heritage into a café on every corner, New Orleans was the epicenter of America's coffee fetish. Anyone wondering why need look no farther than the city's European heritage: New Orleans is heir to French and other continental cultures that all value a substantial brew. And, since most of the coffee beans roasted and ground nation-wide came in from Latin America and the Caribbean through the city's storied wharves, the coffee supply was able to meet the significant demand. The fact is, a century before the Irish started drinking Irish coffee, the French, Spanish, Italians, Germans, Greeks, and Croatians of the Big Easy were busy turning their starter fluid into a good stiff drink.

{coffee drinks}

Irish Coffee

According to most folks, Irish coffee was created by a bartender at Shannon Airport in Ireland, but around New Orleans, we prefer to think that it was created in the Irish Channel, that rough-and-tumble working-class neighborhood just a cabbage throw from the Mississippi. And since cabbages are *indeed* thrown during the neighborhood's annual green-beer-swilling St. Patrick's Day parade, folks have had plenty of time to test this bit of Crescent City physics. Not us, mind you. But we've heard over Irish coffee that it's totally true.

1 1/4 ounces Jameson Irish whiskey

4 ounces freshly brewed hot coffee

Freshly whipped heavy cream

Combine the whiskey and coffee in an Irish coffee glass and top with a dollop of the whipped cream.

Recommended Listening: Wynton Marsalis, "Father Time"

Cognac Café au Lait

We like to think that in the old days, New Orleans consumed most of the brandy made in the Cognac region of France. That's what it seems like from the history books anyway. And one of the simplest, most traditional, and best ways to enjoy a good cognac is with your coffee at the end of a great New Orleans meal. Count Arnaud Cazenave of Arnaud's used to alternate drinking cognac and black coffee throughout each long night working at his restaurant, consuming more than 20 cups of each, it is said. This recipe saves you the trouble of counting accurately as you switch between the two. By the way, in New Orleans we always prefer a blend of coffee and chicory, a stretch introduced during the austerity of the Civil War and kept around because we learned to love the flavor.

3 ounces hot brewed coffee and chicory blend

3 ounces scalded milk

1 teaspoon sugar

1$^{1}/_{4}$ ounces cognac

Combine the coffee and scalded milk in a coffee cup or any tempered glassware. Stir in the sugar, then the cognac.

♛ Recommended Listening:
Art Neville, "All These Things"

Cocoa Nut Café

No, this isn't the name of a new "quick casual" restaurant concept—though, now that we're thinking about it . . . It's actually a terrific coffee drink given depth of flavor by chocolate, hazelnut, and cream. There's a lot to love in this particular mug of java.

$^1/_2$ ounce Bailey's Irish Cream

$^1/_2$ ounce Frangelico hazelnut liqueur

$^1/_2$ ounce Godiva dark chocolate liqueur

Coffee

Whipped cream (optional)

Pour the Bailey's, hazelnut liqueur, and chocolate liqueur into a coffee mug. Fill with hot coffee and stir to blend. Top with whipped cream.

♛ **Recommended Listening:** Spencer Bohren, "Night Is Falling"

Heavenly Iced Coffee

One of the nicest things to happen to coffee in recent years—hastened along by those places that like to sell you a cup for $4—is the popular embrace of iced coffee. People in the South have drunk iced coffee for generations, especially in the summer, when it's just too damn hot to drink it the conventional way. Now, however, you could almost write a cookbook filled with all the great iced coffee recipes. This spiked version of iced coffee warms you up, even while it's cooling you down.

> **4 ounces brewed coffee, cooled**
>
> **1 ounce Kahlúa**
>
> **$3/4$ ounce Nocello walnut liqueur**
>
> **$3/4$ ounce Bailey's Irish Cream**

Combine all the ingredients and shake with ice. Strain into a 10-ounce glass, preferably a paneled Gibraltar glass, over fresh ice.

♛ **Recommended Listening:** Dave Williams, "The Same Old Love"

Café Brulot Diabolique

No book of drinks from New Orleans should leave out café brulot. Some recipes shortchange you on the theater, just bubbling all the ingredients together in a bowl until the flavors get all friendly. In this recipe we call *diabolique* ("in the style of the devil"), we explain the whole show, as it's performed many times each night in dining rooms all over New Orleans. The tradition is to serve this coffee drink in brulot cups, a variation of demitasse with a depiction of a suave and grinning Satan on the side. Be confident but careful with this one. Like so many other things we associate with the devil, it definitely involves playing with fire.

> **2 tablespoons whole cloves**
>
> **14 cinnamon sticks, broken**
>
> **2 tablespoons sugar**
>
> **Thinly sliced peel of 1 lemon**
>
> **1 orange**
>
> **$1/2$ cup plus 1 tablespoon Grand Marnier**
>
> **$1/3$ cup plus 1 tablespoon cognac**
>
> **4 cups hot coffee**

Place the cloves, cinnamon sticks, sugar, and lemon peel in a large heat-proof bowl. Carefully peel the orange, keeping the peel in one large twisting piece. Stud the orange peel with the cloves and rewrap the peel around the orange. Place the orange in the bowl. Add $1/2$ cup of the Grand Marnier and $1/3$ cup of the cognac, then set the bowl over a small flame or Sterno fire until all the ingredients are heated through. Remove the orange from the bowl with a fork.

Pour the remaining 1 tablespoon Grand Marnier and 1 tablespoon cognac into a silver or stainless-steel ladle and ignite it carefully using a long-stemmed match. With your other hand, pick up the orange and let the peel unfurl down until it almost touches the liquid in the bowl. Have someone dim the lights in the room. Slowly pour the flaming liquid from the ladle onto the orange so that it flows down the clove-studded orange peel into the bowl, igniting that liquid. Scoop the flaming liquid from the bowl once or twice with the ladle and pour it down the peel. When the flames are extinguished, pour the coffee into the bowl. Ladle the drink into New Orleans brulot cups or any decorative coffee cups. Serves 6.

♛ **Recommended Listening:** James Rivers, "Second Line"

COFFEE DRINKS

Café l'Orange

Not one but two of the liqueurs used in this cocktail carry more than a hint of orange peel—both the Cointreau and the famous French orange brandy Grand Marnier. And in case anybody wonders what that wonderful taste might be, we throw in the orange peel as a big hint.

$1/2$ ounce Cointreau

$1/2$ ounce Grand Marnier

$1/2$ ounce Godiva dark chocolate liqueur

Coffee

1 thinly sliced orange peel, for garnish

Pour the Cointreau, Grand Marnier, and chocolate liqueur into a coffee mug. Fill with hot coffee and stir to combine. Garnish with the orange peel.

♔ **Recommended Listening:** The Subdudes, "Sugar Pie"

The phrase "nonalcoholic cocktail" may sound like an oxymoron, and that's because it is. Be that as it may, at least two cultural forces have pushed these strange creations to the fore. One is the new emphasis on moderation, which, for all the snide remarks you're likely to hear in the French Quarter, is actually a good idea. The other is the current popularity of cocktails made with clear, virtually flavorless spirits and that get their flavor from everything else in the glass. Let's face it, except for the kick, "virgin" versions of a lot of contemporary drinks taste as good as the ones with octane. For those who don't drink at all or those who just need a breather in the middle of a long night, the following recipes will offer a safe haven.

{nonalcoholic drinks}

Dreamsicle

Whatever happened to those wonderful ice-cream-on-a-stick things that tasted like oranges, perhaps if oranges could grow on Mars? This drink that conjures up their flavor lets us relive our childhoods each time we take a sip. And because it's nonalcoholic, we can share this treat with youngsters who perhaps have never chased an ice cream truck down the street on a lazy, hazy summer day.

4 ounces freshly squeezed orange juice

1³/₄ ounces heavy cream

³/₄ ounce grenadine

Lemon-lime soda

1 maraschino cherry, for garnish

1 orange slice, for garnish

Combine the orange juice, cream, and grenadine and shake with ice. Strain into a Hurricane glass filled with fresh crushed ice. Top with the soda, stir, and garnish with the cherry and orange slice.

Recommended Listening: Jimmy Clanton, "Just a Dream"

Tropical Storm

New Orleans, while not officially in the Tropics, has a lot of tropical storms. Some are the type that are featured on the Weather Channel, the kind that tend to grow up and become hurricanes when they suck up the warm waters of the Gulf of Mexico. Others just bring a little rain on a summer afternoon—sometimes only on one block or on one side of a street. This warm, wet weather and this booze-free charmer are about as tropical as you can get.

1³/₄ ounces cranberry juice

1³/₄ ounces freshly squeezed orange juice

1³/₄ ounces pineapple juice

1 ounce sour mix

1 orange slice, for garnish

1 maraschino cherry, for garnish

Combine all the juices and the sour mix and shake with ice. Strain into a Hurricane glass with fresh crushed ice and garnish with the orange slice and cherry.

Recommended Listening: Chief Jolley, "Meet de Boys on de Battlefield"

Barq's Root Beer Float

There's some question about whether the soft drink called Barq's created in New Orleans is a true root beer or not. The real question is: does anybody think we care? To New Orleanians, Barq's is the only root beer—even now that it has moved away and been acquired by Pepsi.

3 scoops premium vanilla ice cream

1 (12-ounce) bottle Barq's root beer

Place the ice cream in a 22-ounce highball glass and pour the Barq's on top. Serve with a straw and spoon.

♔ Recommended Listening: Annie Laurie, "Since I Fell for You"

NONALCOHOLIC DRINKS

Sweet Tea

You probably won't find the "sweet tea" beloved across the Deep South from Texas to Georgia in most cafés and other casual eateries in New Orleans, and we demand to know why. It's probably because everybody's mother used to make the wonderful stuff, and maybe they still do. The key is adding simple syrup, which is much easier than trying to dissolve something like 1,218 teaspoons of sugar in the brew.

10 ounces brewed ice tea

2 ounces simple syrup (page 15)

1 lemon wedge, for garnish

Pour the tea and simple syrup over ice in a 22-ounce highball glass. Stir and garnish with the lemon wedge.

♔ Recommended Listening: Ernie K-Doe, "Te-Ta-Te-Ta-Ta"

Lemonade

There's nothing better than sitting out under the trees during a New Orleans summer, sipping from a glass filled with plenty of ice and this lemonade.

¹/₂ cup simple syrup (page 15)

¹/₂ cup freshly squeezed lemon juice

1 cup cold water

Sugar

Pour simple syrup, lemon juice, and water into a 22-ounce highball glass with a sugared rim. Stir gently and serve.

Recommended Listening: Dr. John, "Gris-Gris Gumbo Ya-Ya"

Fruit Smoothie

Here's one of the few drinks that's good for you and, conveniently, will also cure hangovers. This is our favorite fruit smoothie, but using just about any other fruit you can think of would probably be great, too.

¹/₂ banana

2 ounces milk or heavy cream

1¹/₄ ounces fresh strawberry puree

1¹/₄ ounces fresh mango puree

1¹/₄ ounces fresh raspberry puree

1 strawberry, for garnish

Combine the banana, milk, and fruit purees in a blender and blend until smooth. Pour into a stemmed glass and garnish with the strawberry.

Recommended Listening: Branford Marsalis, "No Backstage Pass"

Big Easy
Snacks

Oysters and Bacon Brochettes

Makes 36 brochettes | In New Orleans, one of the classic oyster appetizers—right up there with oysters Rockefeller—is called oysters *en brochette*. In our version, we not only spice up the traditional skewer of batter-fried oysters and bacon, but we also pair it with another New Orleans classic, *ravigote*. Best known as a kind of mayonnaise-based crabmeat salad, ravigote, to us, is a cold sauce just dying for an introduction to our hot fried oysters.

RAVIGOTE

3 cups high-quality mayonnaise

2 tablespoons Creole mustard

2 tablespoons prepared horseradish

1 tablespoon capers, drained and rinsed

1 teaspoon freshly squeezed lemon juice

1 teaspoon white vinegar

$^1/_2$ teaspoon roasted garlic puree (page 127)

$^1/_4$ teaspoon Worcestershire sauce

$^1/_4$ teaspoon hot pepper sauce

$^1/_8$ teaspoon black pepper

$^1/_8$ teaspoon white pepper

$^1/_8$ teaspoon Angel Dust seasoning blend (page 124)

12 slices extra-thick bacon

3 dozen oysters

Angel Dust seasoning blend (page 124)

Canola oil, for deep-frying

4 eggs, beaten

2 tablespoons water

5 cups seasoned corn flour (page 126)

TO MAKE THE RAVIGOTE, whisk together all the ingredients in a large bowl.

TO PREPARE THE OYSTERS, cook the bacon in a skillet over medium-low heat until it just starts to crisp, 6 to 8 minutes. Remove from the heat and drain on paper towels. Cut each bacon slice into 3 pieces. Wrap each oyster in a piece of bacon and thread each onto a skewer. Season with Angel Dust.

POUR THE OIL INTO A FRYING PAN to a depth of about 5 inches. Heat until the oil reaches 350°F on a deep-frying thermometer.

MEANWHILE, IN A BOWL, stir the beaten eggs with the water. Spread the corn flour in a shallow dish. Dip each oyster into the corn flour, then into the egg wash, and then into the flour again. Deep-fry until golden brown, about 3 minutes. Do not overcook. Sprinkle with additional Angel Dust, if desired, and serve with the cold ravigote on the side.

Chicken and Andouille Quesadilla with Cilantro Sour Cream

Makes 8 wedges | Even though the quesadilla was introduced to the United States via Mexico and traditionally features the flavors of that cuisine, it is arguably just a delicious delivery system for anything you want to mix in with the mandatory cheese inside. Here we increase the one layer of cheese filling to two, also upping the tortillas from two to three per quesadilla. When you taste this Cajun-influenced version with chicken and andouille, you'll be happy it's a high-rise!

SNACKS

CILANTRO SOUR CREAM

$1/2$ cup sour cream, preferably Mexican-style crema

1 teaspoon finely chopped cilantro

$1/8$ teaspoon garlic powder

3 large (10-inch) flour tortillas

1 cup diced grilled chicken breast

1 cup diced grilled andouille

1 red bell pepper, roasted, peeled, and diced

$3/4$ cup grated Chihuahua or Monterey Jack cheese

$3/4$ cup grated jalapeño Chihuahua or pepper Jack cheese

2 tablespoons extra-virgin olive oil

$1/4$ teaspoon ground guajillo or jalapeño chile

TO MAKE THE CILANTRO SOUR CREAM, stir all the ingredients together in a bowl. Cover and refrigerate until needed.

PLACE A TORTILLA ON A PLATE and top with about half the chicken, andouille, roasted bell pepper, and cheeses, then cover with another tortilla. Spread the remaining fillings on top and cover with the third tortilla. In a bowl, stir together the olive oil with the ground guajillo chile and brush some of the mixture on top of the quesadilla.

CAREFULLY TRANSFER THE QUESADILLA, oiled side down, to a nonstick pan over medium heat. Brush the second side with the oil-chile mixture and cook, flipping once carefully, until both sides are golden brown and the cheese is melted, 5 to 6 minutes per side. Transfer the quesadilla to a large plate and cut into 8 wedges. Serve with the cilantro sour cream.

Open-Faced Hot Muffaletta

Makes 16 pieces | Way back around 1900, some enterprising Sicilian working near the French Market decided to go ahead and do what he kept seeing his customers do with the cold cuts, cheese, olive salad, and big, round loaves of crusty bread called *muffaletta* that they bought. The rest, as they say, is history—except that we just came up with a way to make an even better muffaletta that's perfect for serving as party food or part of a buffet. We love the fact that it's served hot (as the original was not), which of course makes the cheese all melty. You can take a shortcut by buying olive salad in a jar, but after you taste this version we don't think you will.

JIMMY'S OLIVE SALAD

1 cup pitted and coarsely chopped large green Greek olives

1 cup pitted and coarsely chopped manzanilla olives with pimentos

1 (15.5-ounce) jar Italian giardiniera (pickled vegetables), drained and chopped

1/2 cup plus 1 tablespoon extra-virgin olive oil

1 tablespoon minced fresh parsley

1 tablespoon roasted garlic puree (page 127)

2 teaspoons capers, drained and rinsed

1/2 teaspoon dried oregano

1/8 teaspoon salt

1/8 teaspoon black pepper

1/8 teaspoon white pepper

continued

¹/₈ teaspoon crushed red pepper flakes

1 (15-inch) loaf French bread

¹/₄ pound sliced Genoa salami

³/₄ pound sliced provolone cheese

¹/₄ pound sliced baked ham

¹/₄ pound sliced mortadella

TO MAKE THE OLIVE SALAD, combine all the ingredients in a large bowl. Cover and let marinate in the refrigerator for at least 4 hours before using.

PREHEAT THE OVEN to 350°F.

TO ASSEMBLE THE SANDWICH, slice the French bread in half lengthwise. Lay the halves, cut side up, on a baking sheet and spread with the olive salad, using about 1 cup total; reserve the remainder in the refrigerator for another use. Divide the salami between the two halves, arranging it evenly over the bread. Repeat with half of the provolone, all of the ham, and all of the mortadella. Top with the remaining provolone. Drizzle with a bit of the olive oil from the olive salad, if desired.

BAKE UNTIL THE CHEESE IS MELTED, about 10 minutes, then increase the heat to broil and broil until the tops turn golden brown, 2 to 3 minutes. Slice each half into 8 pieces and serve warm.

Grilled Andouille with Honey Creole Mustard Sauce

Serves 6 to 8 as an appetizer | In France, *andouille* refers to any of a wide variety of smoked sausages. In south Louisiana, however, it's a fairly specific blend of meat, smoke, and spice. Although cooks used to have to improvise, using any old smoked sausage or even Polish kielbasa when a Creole or Cajun recipe called for andouille (talk about fusion!), you can now easily buy the real thing online or by mail order.

> **1$^1/_2$ cup Creole mustard**
> **1$^3/_4$ tablespoons honey**
> **1 pound andouille**

PREPARE A GRILL for cooking over medium-high heat.

MEANWHILE, TO PREPARE THE SAUCE, combine the mustard and honey in a saucepan and heat over medium-low heat until warm and bubbling. Remove from the heat and set aside.

USING A FORK, poke a few holes in each andouille link to allow the steam to escape, then grill over medium-high heat until striped with grill marks, about 10 minutes. Slice the andouille into rounds $^1/_2$ inch thick and serve with the mustard sauce.

Catfish Bites with Homemade Tartar Sauce

Makes 56 to 64 catfish bites | Time was, catfish was what you got on the hook when you really wanted trout, redfish, or pompano. With the rise of fish farming in Mississippi and elsewhere in the South, mild, flaky catfish has become one of America's favorite fish. You can do all kinds of weird stuff with it, from soup to stir-fries, but we find it hard to beat our bite-sized version of fried catfish with tartar sauce.

SNACKS

TARTAR SAUCE

²/₃ cup mayonnaise

4 teaspoons sweet pickle relish

4 teaspoons finely chopped Spanish green olives

2 teaspoons minced green onions

¹/₂ teaspoon minced fresh parsley

¹/₂ teaspoon freshly squeezed lemon juice

¹/₈ teaspoon Worcestershire sauce

¹/₈ teaspoon hot pepper sauce

¹/₈ teaspoon Angel Dust seasoning blend (page 124)

¹/₈ teaspoon dried dill

¹/₈ teaspoon ground red pepper

Canola oil, for deep-frying

4 (8-ounce) catfish fillets, each cut into 14 to 16 bites

2 teaspoons Angel Dust seasoning blend (page 124)

2 eggs, beaten

1 teaspoon water

Seasoned corn flour (page 126)

continued

TO MAKE THE TARTAR SAUCE, combine all the ingredients in a bowl. Cover and refrigerate for at least 1 hour.

POUR THE OIL into a frying pan to a depth of about 5 inches. Heat until the oil reaches 350°F on a deep-frying thermometer.

TO PREPARE THE FISH, season the catfish pieces with the Angel Dust. In a bowl, stir the eggs with the water. Spread the corn flour in a shallow dish. Dredge the catfish pieces first in the corn flour, then in the egg wash, and then in the flour again. Deep-fry until golden brown, 3 to 4 minutes. Drain on paper towels and serve with the tartar sauce on the side.

Chargrilled Oysters
with Garlic Butter

Makes 24 oysters | This oyster dish harks back to simpler times in south Louisiana, when the oystermen—almost always Croatians—might pull up on some lonely beach and slap the only thing they had for dinner on a little coal fire. According to one story, during the Great Depression, Croatian oystering families ate nothing but the bivalves for breakfast, lunch, and dinner. We know that if we had to do that, this incredible recipe would be a highlight of our week for sure.

GARLIC BUTTER

6 tablespoons unsalted butter, at room temperature

4 teaspoons grated Asiago cheese

2 teaspoons roasted garlic puree (page 127)

$1/2$ teaspoon chopped fresh parsley

$1/8$ teaspoon salt

$1/8$ teaspoon black pepper

24 oysters on the half shell

Angel Dust seasoning blend (page 124)

TO MAKE THE GARLIC BUTTER, combine all the ingredients in a bowl, mashing with the back of the spoon so that everything is evenly mixed into the softened butter.

PREPARE A GRILL for cooking over medium-high heat.

TOP EACH OYSTER with about 1 teaspoon of the garlic butter, then sprinkle lightly with Angel Dust. Set the shells on the preheated grill and cook until the butter is melted and bubbling, 2 to 3 minutes.

Crawfish Popcorn Mini Po-Boys with Cayenne Mayo

Makes 10 small po-boys | A few years back, fried crawfish tails came to be known as "Cajun popcorn"—we presume because you can just pop them into your mouth. Or maybe it refers to that fact that once you get started popping these things, you just can't seem to stop. You guys can argue among yourselves about what the name really means, but we expect our mouths will be too full of these mini po-boys to talk.

CAYENNE MAYO

1/4 cup mayonnaise

1/8 teaspoon ground red pepper

1/8 teaspoon Worcestershire sauce

1/8 teaspoon white pepper

1/2 teaspoon lemon juice

1/8 teaspoon hot pepper sauce

1 (15-inch) loaf French bread

1/2 cup garlic butter (page 91)

Canola oil, for deep-frying

1 pound crawfish tails, rinsed

1/4 cup hot pepper sauce

Seasoned flour (page 125), for dredging

1 tomato, thinly sliced

2 cups shredded lettuce

TO MAKE THE CAYENNE MAYO, thoroughly combine all the ingredients in a bowl.

PREHEAT THE BROILER. Slice the French bread in half lengthwise. Spread the cut halves lightly with the garlic butter. Toast under the broiler just until golden brown. Set aside.

POUR THE OIL into a frying pan to a depth of about 5 inches. Heat until the oil reaches 350°F on a deep-frying thermometer.

IN A BOWL, combine the crawfish tails with the hot pepper sauce and let marinate for about 5 minutes. Spread the seasoned flour in a shallow dish. Dredge the crawfish in the flour, shaking off any excess. Deep-fry the crawfish until golden brown, about 2 minutes. Transfer to paper towels to drain.

SPREAD THE CAYENNE MAYO on both halves of the French bread. Cover one side with the crawfish and the other with the tomato and lettuce. Carefully arrange the tomato-lettuce side on top of the crawfish side. Slice into 10 pieces, secure each piece with a toothpick, and serve.

SNACKS

Shrimp and Andouille Skewers with Creole Mustard Cream

Makes 10 skewers | Using skewers to cook bits of meat and seafood was probably invented somewhere other than the Big Easy, but New Orleanians knew a good thing when they saw it: they're perfect for whipping up party foods, since the skewers come in handy for serving all sorts of savory snacks. Whether you use shrimp, as called for here, or chicken, or something else, it will surely benefit from its close proximity to the smoke, salt, and spice of the andouille sausage. A quick drizzle of Creole mustard cream doesn't hurt either.

CREOLE MUSTARD CREAM

1 1/4 cups heavy cream

2 tablespoons Creole mustard

1 teaspoon roasted garlic puree (page 127)

1/8 teaspoon Worcestershire sauce

1/8 teaspoon hot pepper sauce

1/8 teaspoon salt

1/8 teaspoon white pepper

1/4 teaspoon cornstarch mixed with 1/2 teaspoon water

1 tablespoon unsalted butter

10 fresh jumbo shrimp, peeled

1 (1/2 pound) link andouille, cut into 10 pieces

2 tablespoons Angel Dust seasoning blend (page 124)

2 teaspoons extra-virgin olive oil

continued

TO MAKE THE CREOLE MUSTARD CREAM, whisk together the cream, mustard, garlic puree, Worcestershire, hot sauce, salt, and pepper in a saucepan. Bring the contents to a boil and whisk for 10 to 12 minutes.

STIR IN THE DISSOLVED CORNSTARCH and let thicken for about 30 seconds. Whisk in the butter. Remove from the heat and set aside.

PREPARE A GRILL for cooking over medium-high heat.

THREAD ONE SHRIMP onto each skewer, followed by one piece of andouille. Sprinkle each skewer with Angel Dust and then brush with olive oil. Grill for a total of 3 minutes, turning once. Drizzle with the Creole mustard cream and serve.

Beef Tenderloin Skewers with Heavenly Worcestershire

Makes 16 skewers | At Heaven on Seven, we go to great lengths to produce our own Worcestershire sauce. But since that takes lots of ingredients and more hours than most people have, we set off to turn store-bought Worcestershire into something great, something delicious ... something, well, heavenly. The sauce we spoon over these wonderful beef tenderloin skewers will make you believe in heaven, too.

HEAVENLY WORCESTERSHIRE

1 cup plus 2 tablespoons Worcestershire sauce

$1/2$ cup molasses

$1/4$ cup dark corn syrup

2 tablespoons honey

$1/4$ cup water

1 tablespoon freshly squeezed lemon juice

1 tablespoon white vinegar

2 pounds beef tenderloin, cut into $1/2$-inch cubes

Angel Dust seasoning blend (page 124)

Extra-virgin olive oil, for brushing

TO MAKE THE SAUCE, combine all the ingredients in a saucepan and boil over medium-high heat until the mixture becomes syrupy, about 8 minutes.

PREPARE A GRILL for cooking over medium-high heat.

THREAD THE BEEF CUBES onto 16 skewers, 3 per skewer. Season with Angel Dust and brush lightly with olive oil. Grill until lightly charred, 4 to 6 minutes. Drizzle with the Worcestershire sauce and serve warm.

Jalapeño-Cheddar Blasters with Honey-Jalapeño Dressing

Makes 64 blasters | The whole South loves corn bread, of course, but most people still haven't tasted this dish we've been making at Heaven on Seven for years. We take that same whistle-Dixie corn bread (we prefer the jalapeño-Cheddar kind), cut it into little squares, and then deep-fry them into what we call "Blasters," marrying corn bread to the hush puppy with delicious results.

JALAPEÑO-CHEDDAR CORN BREAD

1^1/$_2$ cups all-purpose flour

1 cup plus 2 tablespoons finely ground corn flour

^{2}/$_3$ cup sugar

5 teaspoons baking powder

^{1}/$_2$ teaspoon salt

1 egg

1^1/$_3$ cups milk

5 tablespoons unsalted butter, melted

1 cup grated Cheddar cheese

3 tablespoons seeded and chopped jalapeños

HONEY-JALAPEÑO DRESSING

^{2}/$_3$ cup mayonnaise

^{1}/$_2$ cup heavy cream

^{1}/$_3$ cup thinly sliced green onions

1^1/$_2$ teaspoons seeded and minced jalapeños

4 teaspoons honey

$1/4$ teaspoon Worcestershire sauce

$1/4$ teaspoon hot pepper sauce

$1/8$ teaspoon black pepper

$1/8$ teaspoon white pepper

$1/8$ teaspoon ground red pepper

Canola oil, for deep-frying

8 eggs, beaten

2 cups unseasoned dried bread crumbs

TO MAKE THE JALAPEÑO-CHEDDAR CORN BREAD, preheat the oven to 350°F and grease an 8 by 8-inch baking pan. In a bowl, combine the flour, corn flour, sugar, baking powder, and salt. In a separate bowl, lightly beat the egg, then whisk in the milk and butter. Combine the wet and dry ingredients, then thoroughly blend in the cheese and jalapeños. Pour into the prepared pan and bake until golden brown, about 50 minutes. Let cool.

TO MAKE THE HONEY-JALAPEÑO DRESSING, whisk the mayonnaise with the cream in a large bowl. Stir in the remaining ingredients, cover, and refrigerate until you are ready to use.

POUR THE OIL into a frying pan to a depth of about 5 inches. Heat until the oil reaches 350°F on a deep-frying thermometer.

SLICE THE COOLED CORN BREAD into sixty-four 1-inch squares. Dip each square into the beaten egg, then coat lightly with the bread crumbs. Deep-fry until golden brown, 2 to 3 minutes. Drain on paper towels and serve hot with the honey-jalapeño dressing on the side.

Chicken and Andouille Lettuce Wraps

Makes 14 to 16 wraps | The more we came to love those Asian appetizers consisting of spiced ground pork that diners roll up themselves in delicate lettuce leaves, the more we thought New Orleans should have a version all its own. We kept some of the signature Asian flavors, like soy sauce and sesame oil, but the andouille is just about as New Orleans as you can get. Be sure to taste the filling and adjust the seasonings. If the andouille you're using is on the salty side, you may need to reduce the amount of soy sauce, or opt for reduced-sodium soy sauce.

$^1/_4$ **cup sesame oil**

1 pound ground chicken

$^1/_2$ **pound andouille, diced**

1 teaspoon Angel Dust seasoning blend (page 124)

$^1/_2$ **cup diced yellow onion**

$^1/_2$ **cup diced green bell pepper**

1 tablespoon roasted garlic puree (page 127)

$^1/_8$ **teaspoon white pepper**

$^1/_8$ **teaspoon black pepper**

$^1/_8$ **teaspoon crushed red pepper flakes**

$^1/_4$ **cup soy sauce**

$^1/_4$ **cup water**

16 Bibb lettuce leaves

HEAT THE SESAME OIL in a sauté pan over high heat. Add the chicken and cook until browned, about 4 minutes, then add the andouille, stirring until it starts to crisp, about 5 minutes more. Season with the Angel Dust. Stir in the onion, bell pepper, and garlic puree, along with the white and black pepper and red pepper flakes. Stir in the soy sauce and water and deglaze the pan, stirring to scrape up any browned bits from the bottom and sides.

TRANSFER THE MIXTURE to a food processor and pulse 2 or 3 times until it is finely chopped. Serve the mixture in a bowl surrounded by lettuce leaves for wrapping.

Barbecue Shrimp on Corn Bread Squares

Makes 36 squares | Here is one of our favorite discoveries. We take the buttery-peppery barbecue shrimp that have become a modern classic in New Orleans, and then we serve them atop squares of wonderful corn bread. Talk about a marriage made in heaven!

> 1 pan corn bread (page 98)
>
> 36 jumbo shrimp, peeled
>
> 3 teaspoons Angel Dust seasoning blend (page 124)
>
> 3 cups unsalted butter
>
> $1^1/_2$ cups Abita Turbodog or other dark beer
>
> 3 teaspoons black pepper
>
> 3 teaspoons white pepper
>
> $^3/_4$ cup Worcestershire sauce
>
> 3 tablespoons roasted garlic puree (page 127)
>
> $^3/_4$ cup heavy cream

PREPARE THE CORN BREAD according to the recipe on page 98, omitting the jalapeño and Cheddar. Slice the cooled corn bread into 36 squares.

SEASON THE SHRIMP with the Angel Dust and set aside.

HEAT THE BUTTER in a large skillet over high heat. Stir in the beer, peppers, Worcestershire, garlic puree, and heavy cream. Reduce the mixture until thickened and creamy, 5 to 7 minutes. Add the shrimp and cook in the sauce just until pink, about 4 minutes. Spoon one shrimp and plenty of sauce over each corn bread square and serve at once.

Grilled Creole-Spiced Scallops with Citrus-Cilantro Gris-Gris

Makes 12 skewers | There was a time New Orleanians preferred small, delicate bay scallops, but when those started playing hard to get, larger sea scallops became popular. We like "day boat" scallops, brought in and quickly shipped out each day. And since the sweet flavor of scallops is so extraordinary all by itself, we like to hold back on that traditional New Orleans blast of flavor. A little Angel Dust will do for grilling, followed by the Citrus-Cilantro Gris-Gris we created just for this purpose. And *gris-gris*, of course, means a voodoo potion or magic spell in Louisiana Creole-Cajun French.

^{1}/$_2$ cup cilantro leaves

^{1}/$_4$ cup freshly squeezed lemon juice

^{1}/$_4$ cup freshly squeezed orange juice

1 tablespoon honey

1 teaspoon roasted garlic puree (page 127)

^{1}/$_4$ teaspoon salt

^{1}/$_8$ teaspoon white pepper

^{1}/$_8$ teaspoon black pepper

1 cup extra-virgin olive oil, plus more for brushing

24 sea scallops

Angel Dust seasoning blend (page 124)

SNACKS

IN A BLENDER, combine the cilantro, citrus juices, honey, garlic puree, salt, and peppers and puree until smooth. With the blender running on high speed, slowly drizzle in 1 cup of the olive oil, blending until the mixture is emulsified. Set aside.

PREPARE A GRILL for cooking over medium-high heat.

SEASON THE SCALLOPS with Angel Dust. Thread one scallop onto two parallel skewers (this will make them easier to turn on the grill). Thread another scallop onto the two skewers, so that there are two scallops on each pair of skewers. Repeat with the remaining scallops and skewers. Brush lightly with olive oil. Grill just until firm, 5 to 7 minutes. Transfer to a serving platter, drizzle with the gris-gris, and serve.

Crawfish Crescents

Makes 32 crescents | Sometimes, we're not interested in the "pursuit of happiness" so much as the "pursuit of easiness," and on days like that we appreciate this dish, in which our delicious crawfish filling delivers great taste to those refrigerated crescent rolls sold in every supermarket. If you're suddenly stuck fixing hors d'oeuvres for people who are already on their way, turn to these quick and easy crescents. Your guests will think you worked all day!

6 tablespoons unsalted butter

$1/4$ cup diced celery

$1/4$ cup diced green bell pepper

1 tablespoon diced red onion

1 tablespoon diced white onion

1 tablespoon chopped green onions

2 teaspoons roasted garlic puree (page 127)

1 pound crawfish tails, rinsed and chopped

$1/8$ teaspoon crushed red pepper flakes

$1/8$ teaspoon white pepper

$1/8$ teaspoon black pepper

1 teaspoon Angel Dust seasoning blend (page 124)

1 cup grated Asiago cheese

$1/2$ cup grated mozzarella

4 packages refrigerated crescent rolls
   (making 8 rolls each)

TO MAKE THE CRAWFISH STUFFING, melt the butter in a sauté pan over medium-high heat. Add the celery, bell pepper, all the onions, and the garlic puree and sauté just until the vegetables are softened. In a bowl, mix the crawfish tails with the peppers and the Angel Dust. Add the crawfish tails to the pan and sauté for about 5 minutes. Set aside to cool. Mix in the Asiago and mozzarella cheeses.

PREHEAT THE OVEN to 375°F.

UNROLL THE REFRIGERATED CRESCENT ROLLS into long triangles. Spread the cooled crawfish stuffing across the long side of each triangle, then roll up the pastry from that side around the stuffing to enclose the stuffing. Place the rolls on an ungreased cookie sheet and bake until golden brown, 11 to 13 minutes. Serve warm.

Gator Taters

Makes 35 Gator Taters | Honestly, just about everybody loves those cheap thrills called Tater Tots, so we decided to have some fun upgrading them to something even a food snob from New Orleans would admit going crazy for. Naturally, for the dipping sauce, regular boring ketchup had to go, replaced by a version of the Creole sauce New Orleanians love on shrimp, chicken, and whatever else wanders by. For the taters themselves, we took luscious Yukon Gold potatoes, boiled them, mashed them, rolled them, battered them, and fried them. These things are a bit of work—but they're a piece of work as well. The second time you make them, we bet you'll double the recipe.

> 2 cups Creole cocktail sauce (page 116)
>
> 1½ pounds small Yukon Gold potatoes
>
> 1 cup heavy cream
>
> 4 tablespoons unsalted butter
>
> 1 tablespoon roasted garlic puree (page 127)
>
> 1¾ teaspoons salt
>
> ⅛ teaspoon white pepper
>
> Canola oil, for deep-frying
>
> ½ cup grated Cheddar cheese
>
> 3 cups dried bread crumbs
>
> ½ teaspoon Angel Dust seasoning blend (page 124)
>
> 4 eggs, beaten with 2 tablespoons water

CHILL THE COCKTAIL SAUCE in the refrigerator until cold. Puree the sauce in a blender until smooth and keep cold until ready to use.

BOIL THE POTATOES in salted water for 30 minutes and drain. When they are cool enough to handle, peel the potatoes and transfer to a large bowl.

Combine the cream, butter, and garlic puree in a saucepan and heat over medium heat until warm. Slowly add the cream mixture to the potatoes as you mash them, mashing until the potatoes are creamy. Season with $3/4$ teaspoon of the salt and the pepper. Cover the bowl and chill the potatoes in the refrigerator for at least 30 minutes.

POUR THE OIL into a frying pan to a depth of about 5 inches. Heat until the oil reaches 350°F on a deep-frying thermometer.

IN THE CHILLED BOWL, add the cheese to the mashed potatoes. Roll the mixture into 36 small logs, then flatten the ends of each log to make a shape that resembles a barrel. Spread the bread crumbs in a shallow dish and season with the Angel Dust and the remaining 1 teaspoon salt. Coat the potatoes first in the bread crumbs, then in the egg wash, then in the bread crumbs again. Deep-fry until golden brown, about 2 minutes. Drain on paper towels and serve warm with the Creole cocktail sauce.

Coconut-Crusted Chicken with Habanero-Orange Marmalade

Makes 36 skewers | We've loved using coconut as a crispy coating since it became part of the New Orleans repertoire, probably borrowed from Asian or Hawaiian cuisine. Wherever the idea came from, the tropical touch is perfect for New Orleans taste buds. In this recipe, featuring skewered strips of chicken that make the perfect party food, we prefer to use shredded coconut that's been toasted for a few minutes in a 300°F oven, but even if you use the coconut straight out of the bag, you should be happy enough when these skewers come out of the fryer. They quickly make their way toward our orange marmalade, given a kick by a close encounter with habanero peppers.

HABANERO-ORANGE MARMALADE

3 (10-ounce) jars good-quality orange marmalade

3 tablespoons freshly squeezed orange juice

3 teaspoons Heavenly Blend or other habanero pepper sauce

Canola oil for deep-frying

6 (6-ounce) chicken breasts

3 cups seasoned flour (page 125)

5 cups toasted coconut

4 eggs, beaten with 2 tablespoons water and $1/8$ teaspoon Angel Dust seasoning blend (page 124)

TO MAKE THE MARMALADE, combine all the ingredients thoroughly in a bowl. Set aside.

POUR THE OIL into a frying pan to a depth of about 5 inches. Heat until the oil reaches 350°F on a deep-frying thermometer.

SLICE EACH OF THE CHICKEN BREASTS into 6 strips. Thread each strip onto a skewer. Spread the seasoned flour and the coconut on separate plates or shallow dishes. Dredge each chicken strip in the seasoned flour, then in the egg wash, then in the toasted coconut, making sure they are generously coated. Deep-fry until golden brown, about 3 minutes. Drain on paper towels, transfer to a platter, and serve warm with the marmalade.

SNACKS

Oysters Rockefeller Dip

Makes 4 cups of dip | Oysters Rockefeller, the decadent baked oyster dish created at Antoine's a million years ago and named in honor of its own richness, has inspired dozens of similar recipes featuring oysters baked on the half shell. So, of course, we decided to think outside the shell. This unbelievably good (and very rich) party dip delivers all the flavors of a great New Orleans Rockefeller, thanks to the chopped oysters folded right in.

SNACKS

   1 French baguette

   $1/2$ cup garlic butter (page 91)

   $1/2$ cup unsalted butter

   2 (6-ounce) bags washed baby spinach, chopped

   $1/3$ cup diced yellow onion

   1 tablespoon roasted garlic puree (page 127)

   1 teaspoon Pernod

   $1/8$ teaspoon salt

   $1/8$ teaspoon black pepper

   1 cup heavy cream

   $1/2$ cup grated Parmesan cheese

   1 pint shucked oysters, chopped

   2 teaspoons cornstarch dissolved in 2 teaspoons water

PREHEAT THE BROILER. Slice the baguette into $1/4$-inch-thick slices. Spread the slices lightly with the garlic butter. Toast under the broiler just until golden brown. Set aside.

MELT THE UNSALTED BUTTER in a large saucepan over medium-high heat. Add the spinach, onion, garlic puree, and Pernod and sauté until the spinach is wilted. Season with the salt and pepper. Pour in the cream and reduce over high heat until the mixture is thick, about 6 minutes. Fold in the cheese and the oysters, reduce the heat to low, and continue cooking for about 5 minutes. Stir in the dissolved cornstarch to thicken.

TRANSFER TO A SERVING BOWL and serve warm with slices of the garlic toast for dipping.

Cochon de Lait Mini Po-Boys with Cajun Coleslaw

Makes about 20 mini po-boys | One of the most famous of all Cajun dishes is *cochon de lait*, roast suckling pig. The dish took a long time to find its way to the big city of New Orleans, presumably because it's often cooked on a spit outside. City folks don't always deal well with farm animals, so we took the basic idea of *cochon de lait* and turned it into one of the best mini po-boys you're likely to ever taste.

COLESLAW

$1^{1}/_{2}$ cups mayonnaise

1 cup heavy cream

4 tablespoons honey

$2^{1}/_{2}$ tablespoons sugar

1 tablespoon seeded and minced jalapeño

1 teaspoon salt

$^{1}/_{2}$ teaspoon Angel Dust seasoning blend (page 124)

$^{1}/_{2}$ teaspoon Worcestershire sauce

$^{1}/_{2}$ teaspoon Heavenly Blend or other pepper sauce

$^{1}/_{2}$ teaspoon white pepper

$^{1}/_{4}$ teaspoon black pepper

$^{1}/_{4}$ teaspoon ground red pepper

2 pounds shredded green cabbage

$^{2}/_{3}$ cup chopped green onions

$^{1}/_{2}$ cup shredded carrots

PO-BOYS

1 (6- to 7-pound) pork shoulder roast

2$^1/_2$ teaspoons Angel Dust seasoning blend (page 124)

2 tablespoons roasted garlic puree (page 127)

$^1/_4$ cup extra-virgin olive oil

1 yellow onion, chopped

1 carrot, chopped

1 stalk celery, chopped

4 cups canned onion soup

2 tablespoons all-purpose flour

2 (15-inch) loaves French bread

TO MAKE THE COLESLAW, combine all the ingredients thoroughly in a large bowl, cover, and refrigerate for at least 1 hour.

PREHEAT THE OVEN to 375°F.

TO MAKE THE PO-BOYS, season the pork with the Angel Dust and rub the garlic puree and olive oil onto the roast. Heat a sauté pan over high heat, add the pork roast, and brown the meat on all sides. Remove the meat and add the onion, carrot, and celery, cooking until caramelized, 5 to 8 minutes. Add the flour and 1 cup of the onion soup to the pan and deglaze, stirring to scrape up any browned bits from the bottom. Transfer the meat and the vegetables to a roasting pan with a lid, pour in the remaining 3 cups onion soup, cover, and place in the oven. Roast until the meat can be shredded with a fork, 3 to 3$^1/_2$ hours.

TO ASSEMBLE THE PO-BOYS, use two forks to shred the pork into small pieces. Pour the sauce from the pan through a fine-mesh sieve and combine the strained sauce in a bowl with the shredded pork. Slice the French bread in half lengthwise and cut each piece into 10 sections. Cover the bottom pieces of bread with the shredded pork and top with the coleslaw and the remaining pieces of bread. Serve warm.

Spicy Boiled Shrimp with Creole Cocktail Sauce

Makes about 50 shrimp | One of the oldest and most beloved foods for celebrating in New Orleans is boiled shrimp, and plenty of them. In many families, whenever shrimp were the least bit in season, sold from the backs of pickup trucks along the highway, this was the menu served each and every Friday night, when Catholics were required to abstain from eating meat. The Vatican has eased up a good deal on the need to go without meat—but don't try telling that to anybody who really loves our recipe for boiled shrimp, not to mention our recipe for a pungent cocktail sauce that will make you burn through shrimp, salty crackers, and anything else you can think of to dip, dunk, or dredge.

CREOLE COCKTAIL SAUCE

3 cups ketchup

2 tablespoons prepared horseradish

2 tablespoons lemon juice

2 teaspoons Worcestershire sauce

4 quarts water

3 tablespoons powdered seafood boil seasoning, plus more for sprinkling

1 lemon, cut into wedges

1 orange, cut into wedges

2 bay leaves

1 tablespoon black peppercorns

1 tablespoon roasted garlic puree (page 127)

5 pounds (about 50) jumbo shrimp, peeled

TO MAKE THE COCKTAIL SAUCE, combine all the ingredients in a bowl and chill in the refrigerator until ready to use.

TO MAKE THE SHRIMP, in a large pot, bring the water and 3 tablespoons of the seafood boil seasoning to a boil. Squeeze the lemon and orange wedges into the water and add the rinds, bay leaves, peppercorns, and garlic puree. Let boil for 5 minutes, then add the shrimp. Return the water to a boil and cook the shrimp for 2 minutes, just until pink. Do not over-cook. Drain the shrimp and sprinkle with additional seafood boil, mixing well with a large spoon. Refrigerate until cold. Serve chilled with the cocktail sauce.

Jerk Chicken Skewers with Papaya–Scotch Bonnet Sauce

Makes 36 skewers | We like to think of New Orleans as the northernmost Caribbean island. History certainly supports such a view, considering the population explosion here that resulted from slave revolts in the Caribbean in the late eighteenth century. So much of what we love about New Orleans—the rhythms, the speech patterns, the love of spice, that whole voodoo thing—arrived here with the black and white islanders who doubled the population when they arrived. For this recipe, we take those islanders home for a visit, spicing up our chicken with a marinade the Jamaicans call jerk and then serving the skewers with a sweet-hot sauce.

PAPAYA–SCOTCH BONNET SAUCE

1 teaspoon extra-virgin olive oil

$1/4$ yellow onion, diced

$1/2$ teaspoon seeded and chopped Scotch bonnet pepper

$1/4$ teaspoon roasted garlic puree (page 127)

1 medium papaya, peeled and chopped

2 tablespoons water

1 teaspoon honey

$1/8$ teaspoon salt

$1/8$ teaspoon white pepper

2 tablespoons minced fresh cilantro

6 (6-ounce) chicken breasts

$3/4$ cup jerk marinade (page 128)

3 teaspoons Angel Dust seasoning blend (page 124)

Extra-virgin olive oil, for brushing

TO MAKE THE SAUCE, heat the oil in a sauté pan over medium-high heat and sauté the onions for a minute, then stir in the Scotch bonnet pepper and garlic puree. Transfer the mixture to a blender. Add the papaya, water, honey, salt, and pepper and puree until smooth. Transfer the mixture to a bowl, stir in the cilantro, cover, and refrigerate for at least 30 minutes to allow the flavors to blend.

SLICE EACH CHICKEN BREAST into 6 long strips. Cover the chicken with the jerk marinade and Angel Dust, letting it marinate in the refrigerator for 30 to 45 minutes. Meanwhile, prepare a grill for cooking over medium-high heat.

THREAD EACH CHICKEN STRIP onto a wooden skewer. Brush the chicken lightly with olive oil and grill until golden and striped with grill marks, 3 to 4 minutes. Serve warm with the sauce alongside.

SNACKS

FGT Half Moons with Crabmeat-Lemon Mayo

Makes 50 half moons | "FGT" is our way of saying "fried green tomatoes," that great Southern dish that exploded out of rural Alabama some years back on the strength of a book that begat a movie. Fried green tomatoes are mighty good all by themselves, yet we and a lot of other cooks have spent a lot of time seeking the Holy Grail of a perfect topping for them. Sometimes we use a remoulade, but we've found that this crabmeat-lemon mayo is perfect atop the spicy batter. If you're serving these at the table, go ahead and fry whole tomato slices, but for a party snack, cutting the tomatoes into half moons makes for a nibble that's easy to grab and go.

CRABMEAT-LEMON MAYONNAISE

2 cups mayonnaise

2 tablespoons freshly squeezed lemon juice

2 teaspoons roasted garlic puree (page 127)

$^1/_4$ teaspoon Worcestershire sauce

$^1/_4$ teaspoon lemon zest

$^1/_4$ teaspoon Heavenly Blend or other hot sauce

$^1/_8$ teaspoon white pepper

$^1/_8$ teaspoon salt

1 pound lump crabmeat

$^1/_4$ cup chopped green onions

Canola oil, for deep-frying

2 cups all-purpose flour

3 teaspoons Angel Dust seasoning blend (page 124)

continued

1¹/₂ teaspoons salt

25 (¹/₄-inch) slices green tomato, each cut in half

6 eggs, beaten with 3 tablespoons water

3 cups seasoned dried bread crumbs

TO MAKE THE MAYONNAISE, whisk together all the ingredients except the crabmeat and green onions until thoroughly combined. Gently fold in the crabmeat and onions, being careful not to break up the crabmeat. Refrigerate until ready to use.

POUR THE OIL into a frying pan to a depth of about 5 inches. Heat until the oil reaches 350°F on a deep-frying thermometer.

PUT THE FLOUR in a shallow dish and stir in the Angel Dust and salt. Dip the tomato halves first into the flour, then into the egg wash, and finally into the seasoned bread crumbs. Deep-fry in batches until golden brown, 2 to 3 minutes. Drain on paper towels, arrange the tomatoes on a serving platter, top with the mayonnaise, and serve at once.

This is part of a cookbook where the chef always tells you that you need to make your own demi-glace, your own wild boar stock, or maybe your own duck confit—all with a promise that after a mere 72 hours on the stove, it will be the best thing you ever cooked with. Well, we don't really think that way or cook that way very often either. What follows are a few simple recipes that we believe make sense to keep around your kitchen. Angel Dust, for instance, is our version of the Creole or Cajun seasoning that everybody sells. Other items, like the Garlic Puree, are ways we've perfected over the years for delivering the maximum amount of flavor with the minimum amount of time or effort.

{basic recipes}

Angel Dust Cajun Seasoning

Makes ¹/₂ cup | These days just about every New Orleans chef worth his or her, well, salt markets one or more spice blends. With this blend, all our friends can enjoy the bold Louisiana flavors we serve up every day in our restaurants.

> **3 tablespoons Hungarian paprika**
>
> **1¹/₂ tablespoons Spanish paprika**
>
> **5 teaspoons salt**
>
> **1¹/₄ teaspoons dried thyme**
>
> **1¹/₄ teaspoons dried oregano**
>
> **1 teaspoon white pepper**
>
> **¹/₂ teaspoon dried basil**
>
> **¹/₂ teaspoon ground red pepper**
>
> **¹/₄ teaspoon black pepper**
>
> **¹/₈ teaspoon garlic powder**
>
> **¹/₈ teaspoon onion powder**

THOROUGHLY COMBINE ALL THE INGREDIENTS in a small bowl. Use as needed, storing the remainder in an airtight container for up to 2 months.

Seasoned Flour

Makes 1 1/4 cups | We've found that seasoning the flour we use when sautéing and frying is the best way to infuse a dish with flavor.

> 1 cup all-purpose flour
>
> 3 tablespoons cornstarch
>
> 2 teaspoons Angel Dust seasoning blend (page 124)
>
> 1/4 teaspoon salt
>
> 1/8 teaspoon garlic salt
>
> 1/8 teaspoon onion salt
>
> 1/8 teaspoon black pepper
>
> 1/8 teaspoon white pepper

THOROUGHLY COMBINE ALL THE INGREDIENTS in a bowl. Use as needed, storing the remainder in an airtight container in the refrigerator for up to several months.

Seasoned Corn Flour

Makes 1¹/2 cups | As with regular flour, seasoning corn flour gives our foods a little extra "slap." Corn flour, and its coarser kin cornmeal, give many foods from the Deep South the crunch we crave.

1¹/4 cups corn flour

3 tablespoons cornstarch

1 tablespoon Angel Dust seasoning blend (page 124)

³/4 teaspoon salt

¹/8 teaspoon Hungarian paprika

¹/8 teaspoon Spanish paprika

¹/8 teaspoon onion salt

¹/8 teaspoon garlic salt

¹/8 teaspoon black pepper

¹/8 teaspoon white pepper

THOROUGHLY COMBINE ALL THE INGREDIENTS in a bowl. Use as needed, storing the remainder in an airtight container in the refrigerator for up to 3 weeks.

Roasted Garlic Puree

Makes 1 cup | We like to have plenty of this puree on hand so that we can take advantage of the sweet flavor of caramelized garlic any time we cook.

> **1 cup peeled garlic cloves**
>
> **1 cup extra-virgin olive oil**

PREHEAT THE OVEN to 300°F.

PLACE THE GARLIC CLOVES in a small baking dish and pour in the olive oil, making sure all the cloves are covered. Cover with aluminum foil and roast until light brown, about 1 hour. Strain the garlic, reserving the oil, and puree in a blender, adding a little of the reserved oil if necessary to form a smooth paste. Transfer to a storage container and pour in enough fresh oil to cover. Use as needed, storing the remainder in an airtight container in the refrigerator for up to 10 days. Cover and refrigerate the garlic-infused oil in a separate container for other uses—it's great for sautéing any meat, seafood, or vegetable.

Jerk Marinade

Makes ¾ cup | In Jamaica, jerk seasoning is the coin of the realm, a bright green wonderland of spicy great taste used for the traditional jerk pork served on Boston Beach near Port Antonio. This is a version our customers far from their homes in Jamaica have come to value every bit as much.

2 tablespoons ground allspice

½ teaspoon ground nutmeg

½ teaspoon ground cinnamon

¼ teaspoon ground cloves

½ cup finely chopped green onions

2 tablespoons chopped fresh thyme leaves

2 tablespoons freshly squeezed lemon juice

2 tablespoons canola oil

1 tablespoon seeded and chopped Scotch bonnet
   or habanero pepper

1 tablespoon soy sauce

1 tablespoon dark rum

1½ teaspoons minced garlic

1½ teaspoons peeled and grated fresh ginger

1½ teaspoons honey

1½ teaspoons cane syrup or light molasses

1½ teaspoons black pepper

1 teaspoon dark brown sugar

¾ teaspoon Worcestershire sauce

½ teaspoon habanero pepper sauce

¼ teaspoon salt

⅛ teaspoon crushed red pepper flakes

COMBINE THE ALLSPICE, nutmeg, cinnamon, and cloves in a skillet and heat over medium-low heat until toasted and fragrant, 45 to 60 seconds, being careful not to burn the spices. Transfer to a coffee grinder and grind into a fine powder. Transfer the spices to a blender and add all the remaining ingredients. Puree until smooth and incorporated. Use as needed, storing the remainder in an airtight container in the refrigerator for up to 1 week.

MOVIES

Angel Heart. A dark tale of demonic doings in the city and on the bayou, with Robert De Niro even more evil than usual.

The Big Easy. Dennis Quaid is a New Orleans detective with the wackiest Cajun accent ever concocted. In fact, virtually all the people of New Orleans are portrayed as Cajuns, dancing the two-step and calling each other *cher*.

Cat People. A remake of an older thriller, this film features brooding, luminous shots of the city's scenery, happily enhanced by the presence of Natassja Kinski. Weird, ineffective, and kind of dumb but high-octane anyway, there is something very New Orleans about *Cat People*.

Easy Rider. If you've ever wished you could get high passing a joint around one of those ghostly New Orleans cemeteries, it's probably because you saw *Easy Rider* at too young and impressionable an age. Filled with now-standard American "on the road" iconography, the movie is also filled with some American movie icons—Dennis Hopper, Peter Fonda, and Jack Nicholson, by name.

Interview with the Vampire. When it comes to fulfilling most women's fantasies, Anne Rice ranks high for achievement, penning a story that ended up starring both Tom Cruise and Brad Pitt. Her first novel, and the first of many featuring the vampire Lestat, was actually as much about grief as bloodlust, and the film version suggests that with lots of moody visuals. One of those visuals, by the way, is a very young Kirsten Dunst.

JFK. New Orleanians believe that everything worth knowing about happens in New Orleans. They found an unlikely ally in Oliver Stone, who set his conspiracy-ridden film about the Kennedy assassination, starring Kevin Costner, in the Crescent City. Too bad Stone focused on his grudge against the "military industrial complex" rather than on the local Mafia.

King Creole. Before Elvis Presley became the ultimate schlockmeister of the movies, he made a handful of films that are still worth watching. This New Orleans–based black-and-white drama is loved by locals for its numerous shots of locations now long gone.

Live and Let Die. This James Bond film set in New Orleans and the surrounding swamps is a hoot for its dizzying boat chase, Paul McCartney's infectious Top 40 song, Roger Moore's raised-eyebrow one-liners, Jane Seymour as every guy's favorite fortune-teller, and Geoffrey Holder (he of the wild-eyed, deep-throated laugh) as voodoo's Baron Samedi.

Mandingo. This story about dark dealings on an old plantation features world-class boxer Ken Norton as one of the buffest slaves ever and Perry King as the jealous young master aiming to boil him in oil.

Pretty Baby. Brooke Shields went from child model to movie star with this evocative film about Bellocq (played by Keith Carradine), who uses his camera to pick up Storyville prostitutes. Susan Sarandon is luminous as one of them.

The Savage Bees. If New Orleans hosted a film festival featuring the worst movies ever made—and based on the city's treatment by Hollywood, there's no reason it couldn't—this one would have to be its poster child. Killer bees attack sultry New Orleans, only to die in the chill of the Superdome. The filmmakers obviously didn't realize the New Orleans Saints have exclusive rights to do that.

A Streetcar Named Desire. Local playwright Tennessee Williams captured in his language so many sights and sounds of New Orleans that the shadowy near-fantasy world in the movie directed by Elia Kazan can only make us homesick for a city that never quite was.

READING ROOM

The Awakening, by Kate Chopin. Rediscovered by the 1960s feminist movement, this novel describes a woman's sexual coming of age (in 1899).

City of Night, by John Rechy. This novel of a homosexual hustler—considered shocking when it first appeared in bookstores in 1963—devotes considerable pages to New Orleans.

A Confederacy of Dunces, by John Kennedy Toole. This rollicking tale of a boy, his mother, and a Lucky Dog hotdog cart was not published until after the author's suicide. It eventually won the Pulitzer Prize.

Dead Man Walking, by Sister Helen Prejean. A New Orleans Catholic nun ministering to death row inmates, Prejean gives us a gut-wrenching book that became an even more gut-wrenching movie.

Dinner at Antoine's, by Frances Parkinson Keyes. Though dated in its narrative approach, this book actually inspired Owen Brennan to come up with "Breakfast at Brennan's."

The Feast of All Saints, by Anne Rice. Shortly after creating the vampire Lestat, Rice turned to the "free people of color" in New Orleans of the late nineteenth century, to remarkable effect.

Hotel. Arthur Hailey wrote his behind-the-scenes novel about a hotel in New Orleans, combining elements of the Royal Orleans and the Roosevelt at the time the latter was being taken over by "outsiders" from Fairmont.

Last Car to Elysian Fields, by James Lee Burke. Burke's series devoted to booze-plagued detective Dave Robicheaux is one of the best franchises ever to call New Orleans (and New Iberia) home.

The Moviegoer, by Walker Percy. Child of a Deep South literary dynasty, Percy launched his career with this award winner popular with the New Orleans set. The more books he wrote, the more religious he got. How unusual!

Obituary Cocktail: The Great Saloons of New Orleans, by Kerri McCaffety. It's surprising that nobody thought sooner of chronicling the heart and soul of New Orleans by way of its saloons. The author combines intriguing facts with glorious photos.

Ol' Man Adam an' His Chillun, by Roark Bradford. Penned with lots of "Negro dialect" by a 1930s New Orleans fixture, this book inspired the great play and movie *Green Pastures*.

Prism of the Night, by Katherine Ramsland. In the first serious biography of novelist Anne Rice, Ramsland beat several of Rice's own later, more personal and autobiographical novels such as *Violin*. It's not just about vampires.

Up from the Cradle of Jazz, by Jason Berry, Jonathan Foose, and Tad Jones. Tirelessly researched and set down with no sense of hurry, this books takes you to the heart (and soul, of course!) of local music.

INDEX